Radically Open

Radically Open

Transcending Religious Identity
in an Age of Anxiety

Robert F. Shedinger

CASCADE *Books* · Eugene, Oregon

RADICALLY OPEN
Transcending Religious Identity in an Age of Anxiety

Cascade Books
An Imprint of Wipf and Stock Publishers
199 W. 8th Ave., Suite 3
Eugene, OR 97401

www.wipfandstock.com

ISBN 13: 978-1-62032-042-6

Cataloging-in-Publication data:

Shedinger, Robert F.

Radically open: transcending religious identity in an age of anxiety / Robert F. Shedinger.

x + 134 p.; 23 cm—Includes bibliographical references.

ISBN 13: 978-1-62032-042-6

1. Religion—Philosophy. 2. Anxiety. I. Title.

HM271 .S33 2012

Manufactured in the USA.

For Tina, Amey, and Tyler

Contents

Acknowledgments

No book is written in a vacuum, and the people whose ideas have inspired my thoughts are too numerous to mention. But there are specific people without whose influence this book could not have been written. Since my own struggle with anxiety provides a framework for this book, I must thank Carol Hagen, the first mental health professional who validated my feelings and helped me see I was not going crazy. She was a real godsend. I must also acknowledge the author and Jungian analyst James Hollis. I have never met him personally, but through his writings I feel like I know him as an old friend. He opened to me the world of Jungian psychology and helped me fit the pieces of my life back together as the following pages so well attest.

This book is not just about my own emotional struggles, however. Those struggles merely provide an important experiential background for the development of a larger argument which itself has been influenced by the work of many scholars. Since these conversation partners are referenced in the footnotes I will refrain from mentioning them here. But I do need to acknowledge specific people who have helped me in my understanding of Islam as a lived tradition. The Muslim community's response to my previous book *Was Jesus a Muslim?* has led to a number of new relationships for which I am most grateful. Special thanks are due to Ahmed Afzaal, who recognized the value of my approach to Islam and gave me the confidence to pursue it further. I would also like to thank Mustafa Elturk, Amin Varis, and the other members of the Islamic Organization of North America for their support and friendship. It is because of them that I have been able to interact with the good folks in Islamic Centers in Detroit, Raleigh, Santa Clara, Sacramento, Toronto, Las Vegas, and other places where I have always been welcomed and made to feel at home. If it had not been for the gracious hospitality of Dr. Sayyid Qazi, I would not have seen the Grand

Canyon. Thanks are due as well to Dr. Akbar Ahmed for his always gracious support of my work even when he is busy with his own.

Thanks are also due to my good friend Dr. Zulfiqar Ali Shah, Religious Director of the Islamic Society of Milwaukee and Executive Director of the Fiqh Council of North America. His warmth and friendship (and that of his wife, Amal) have made my family's trips to Milwaukee most pleasant, and his professional collegiality has been truly inspiring.

Thanks to Wipf and Stock Publishers, and especially to Charlie Collier, for their support of this project.

Finally, I thank Tina, Amey, and Tyler for putting up with me as I worked on another book, but also for standing beside me through very difficult times. I owe them a huge debt of gratitude.

Introduction

AMERICA STANDS IN THE throes of an anxiety epidemic, yet Americans live in one of the most religious countries in the world. Shouldn't people with such deep spiritual roots be less vulnerable to emotional suffering? Perhaps this little riddle has not occurred to you before—and if not, I am not really too surprised. The paradoxical relationship between religiosity and mental health in America is rarely, if ever, acknowledged. Perhaps the implications are so disturbing that we ignore the paradox intentionally. But ignore it or not, the paradox is real and worth considering. Resolving the enigma of why levels of anxiety and religiosity seem to be simultaneously surging will reveal disturbing but also ultimately liberating truths about ourselves as individuals and the society in which we live. Let's take a closer look at what is happening.

By all accounts, anxiety is running rampant in America, with mental health professionals now referring to anxiety and its close kin, depression, as the "common colds" of mental health disorders. In fact, anxiety holds the distinction of being the number one complaint driving people to seek mental health treatment, with doctors writing an astonishing one hundred million-plus prescriptions every year for antidepressant and antianxiety medications. One in every 76 Americans is considered disabled by mental illness, with most of this disability being related directly to anxiety and depression.[1] Given this, it is hardly a stretch to refer to the closely related disorders of anxiety and depression as constituting a modern American epidemic. But why is this so, and why now? What are we so anxious and depressed about? Surely there are many stresses and strains involved in modern living, especially during periods of depressed economic activity and high unemployment. But is life in the early twenty-first century really

1. Whitaker, *Anatomy of an Epidemic*, 7.

that much more stressful than it was during earlier times of great social upheaval such as the Civil War or the Great Depression or World War II?

Interestingly, as Americans grow more anxious and depressed, they seem to be growing more religious, also. If we can believe the polls, the vast majority of Americans profess belief in God, more than half believe in biblical creationism rather than evolution, and a significant majority attends some type of religious service on a regular basis. Evangelical megachurches are popping up all over the place, boasting membership numbers in the tens of thousands, while religious language infuses our politics at a level never before seen, with the admonition "God bless the United States of America" becoming the requisite perfunctory ending of every presidential address over the last thirty years. To add to this picture, evangelical Christianity has taken on such a public face that it is now almost completely identified with a single political party.

Now, one might expect such high levels of religiosity to go a long way toward helping resolve the epidemic levels of anxiety and depression, but this is obviously not the case. Why not? Shouldn't people with deep spiritual roots be more relaxed and content with their lives? Shouldn't the belief in a benevolent, omnipotent deity who loves us, surrounds us on all sides with the incredible beauty of creation, and promises us an eternity in paradise dispel some of the anxiety of modern living? In short, if we profess such a deep faith in God, why on earth are we so anxious and depressed?

This paradox stands at the center of this book, but I want to raise the more troubling question of whether the paradox is real or just apparent. Could it be that our surging levels of religiosity, rather than allaying the anxiety epidemic, might actually be fostering it? More specifically, is it possible that the exclusive claims to religious identity that have become such a common way to mark personal identity in contemporary America might actually lead to a trivializing of spirituality and a loss of psychological depth, a situation that leaves us more vulnerable to anxiety and depression? As disturbing as this idea might be, I think it is exactly what is going on.

The great Swiss psychoanalyst Carl Jung many years ago suggested that because the word *anxiety* stems from an Indo-European root meaning narrow (hence the related words *anger* and *angina*, the latter referring to a narrowing of cardiac blood vessels causing chest pain), anxiety may actually result from a view of life that has become too narrow and constricted. The solution, he suggested, lay in our ability to open up to a larger, more expansive framework in which to ground the meaning of our lives. If Jung is right, then we must question whether the surging levels of religiosity that more and more are marked by exclusive claims to religious identity may be narrowing our perspective on life and its meaning rather than expanding it, leaving us more vulnerable to anxiety and depression. I believe this to be the case, and I will therefore defend the provocative claim that the surging levels of overt religiosity so characteristic of modern American society actually exacerbate rather than allay our epidemic levels of anxiety and depression. There is no real paradox at all. There only appears to be one because we naturally recoil from the suggestion that surging levels of religiosity—taken by many to be a positive social outcome—might actually be doing us more harm than good. Recoil if you want, but this is exactly what I am suggesting.

Let me be more specific. It is not so much that religiosity directly causes anxiety; the relationship is actually a good bit more subtle. While anxiety can stem from a variety of causes, I will argue that a significant reason for the current surge in anxiety is the demand to live in a secular world that is rapidly becoming spiritually disenchanted. Secularism has cut us off from an authentic connection to a transcendent reality, narrowing our vision of life and its meaning. Religion, ironically, cannot help us recover this spiritual connection because religion turns out to be the product of the process of secularization that causes the problem in the first place. Engaging in overt acts of religiosity keeps us locked in the disenchanted secular frame, which leaves us more vulnerable to anxiety and depression. Unfortunately, the bad news does not end there. Since religion is a secular concept, it has no moral authority to critique the secular worldview, and this allows the triumphant human ego free rein to chase power and wealth, a situation that authorizes the kinds of unjust economic systems that increase anxiety by locking people into cycles of unending poverty, unemployment, underemployment, and other forms of oppression. But here is the good news. Understanding the seemingly paradoxical relationship between religiosity and mental health may hold the keys to a more humane and sustainable future.

Some clarity is in order here on my use of the terms *religiosity* and *religious identity*. Rather than simply living a life guided by the teachings of a particular religious tradition, it seems that more and more Americans today are engaged in a contest to demonstrate publicly how religious they are. This is often done by metaphorically wearing an exclusive religious identity label as a way to convey a person's principal identity—"I am a Christian (or I am a Muslim) and this is the most important thing you need to know about me." For Christians particularly, wearing a religious identity label is often done literally in the form of T-shirts that loudly announce religious identity claims in all kinds of creative ways (or if not T-shirts, then bumper stickers—*Honk if you love Jesus!*—or those ubiquitous WWJD bracelets).

Perhaps this fascination with religious identity labels is most apparent in our modern political discourse. During the 2008 Presidential election, President Obama's identity as a Christian or a Muslim was much debated and was a critical issue for many voters. Even though the United States Constitution explicitly forbids a religious test for public office, many (or is it most?) people simply will not vote for a Muslim for president, only for a Christian (preferably of the Protestant variety!). In the lead-up the 2012 elections, Mitt Romney's Mormon identity has proved to be a significant issue for evangelical Christian voters who want their president to be a Christian like them. Conversely, secular voters may be biased against conservative Christian candidates simply because they are conservative *Christian* candidates who dare to talk about their faith in political contexts. It no longer seems that a presidential candidate's policy proposals or moral character are the most important criteria for evaluating their fitness for political office. For many people religious identity *is* the key issue. In many ways, religious identity labels are becoming the most important markers of personal identity in contemporary America.

At this point you might be wondering what qualifies me to write a book about religion and mental health. After all, though I do hold a PhD in religious studies and can make a strong claim to expertise in issues related to the study of religion and religious identity, I am not a licensed mental health professional. So why should you listen to anything I have to say about anxiety and depression? This is a fair question. My reply is that I know them intimately. I may claim no formal academic training in the mental health field (beyond my clinical pastoral care practicum in seminary), but I do have something that many licensed psychiatrists and psychologists do not—firsthand experience with anxiety and depression. Like some of you—perhaps (given the statistics) many of you—I am an anxiety sufferer. Twice in my life I have been plunged into the darkness of major anxiety, the second and most recent episode (and I hope the last!) nearly disabling me altogether. My journey through the dark valley of major anxiety taught me many lessons that I could never have learned through formal academic training, though I must be clear that those lessons have made me somewhat critical of much of what passes today for standard mental health intervention. Nevertheless, this is not primarily a book about anxiety. It is rather a book that takes a critical look at how religious identity claims may really function in the world. But my understanding of the latter has been profoundly shaped by my experience with the former. It is simply impossible for me to separate my life as an anxiety sufferer from my life as a scholar of religion, nor do I wish to.

Therefore, to establish the link that I believe exists between religiosity and anxiety, I will need to share my story in some detail. My purpose in doing so is not to indulge myself or to exact sympathy. This has been an extremely painful episode in my life and one I would just as soon forget. Laying it bare in the pages of a book for all to read is far from easy, and I approach this task with considerable trepidation. But it will prove much easier to understand the more theoretical aspects of my argument when they can be applied to a concrete example, and rather than make up hypothetical examples for heuristic purposes, it will be more powerful to work with an actual example from real-life experience. I know no one's story better than my own, and my hope is that you may find aspects of your own story in mine. As we will see, my own experience with anxiety did not stem directly from issues related to religious identity. But what I learned experientially about anxiety led me unexpectedly to think in a whole new way about the enigma standing at the center of this book: why are we so anxious when we are at the same time so religious? I seriously doubt I would have discovered this new way of thinking had I not been plunged into the depths of emotional torment. So my experiential reflections are a crucial part of the larger argument of this book.

Now, in case you are wondering, I have thankfully recovered from my most recent episode of anxiety—at least for now. If you have been unfortunate enough to suffer a major anxiety or depressive episode yourself, perhaps my experience and what I have come to make of it can be of some help to you. This is not meant, however, to be a self-help book. There are plenty of those on the market. Rather, putting my experience with anxiety into conversation with my work as a religion scholar, I believe, reveals profound insights into what it means to be human in an age that is rapidly becoming dehumanized and dehumanizing. If you are helped by reading this book, great! But my real goal is to address deeper and more troubling questions about the very foundations of modern American society and its fascination with overt displays of religiosity—one of the characteristics that is said to set America apart from other parts of the Western world where religion seems to be rapidly disappearing (though this characterization is questionable).

Returning to the apparent paradox at the center of this book, what might the solution be to epidemic levels of anxiety and depression if the kind of overt religiosity characterized by exclusive claims to religious identity turns out to be contributing to the problem? My own experience resonates deeply with Jung's understanding of anxiety's cause and its solution, and so I have titled this book *Radically Open: Transcending Religious Identity in an Age of Anxiety*. If the exclusive claims to religious identity we so often make are not resolving our anxieties, and may even be fostering them, then perhaps it is time to move past those narrowly constructed religious identities and open ourselves to a deeper and more expansive spirituality that lies beyond them. Religious communities as they are currently constructed may play an important role in contemporary society, lending some semblance of order and cohesion to people's lives; I am not necessarily advocating that we drop out of our church, mosque, synagogue, or temple. But we must realize that religious communities and the institutional structures that embody them are human creations and should not be understood as guardians of the absolute truth about who we really are, as if the statement "I am a Christian" defines my fundamental identity as a human being—the most important thing about me. Absolute truth, if it exists at all, cannot be grasped by our finite minds, and it clearly transcends the worldview of any human-created tradition or institution—religious ones included. If, therefore, we can develop a sense of personal identity that is deeper than and not tied to any particular religious identity claim, I am convinced that we will be happier and less anxious and that our world will become a more civilized, humane, and just place to live.

What does it really mean to live a radically open life? And how will living such a life lead to a more humane world? It will require several steps to arrive at an answer to these questions. The societal changes underwriting our anxiety epidemic have a long and complicated history. It will take a bit of work to untangle the strands of this complex web. But I assure you the effort will be worthwhile. Let me lay out here a brief summary of the path that lies ahead.

I begin in chapter 1 with a fairly detailed narrative of my own struggles with anxiety and depression in order to show how a Jungian perspective on human psychological development helped me make sense of this experience. With this as a framework, I will then turn in chapter 2 to the question of how we got to the point where exclusive claims to religious identity have come to play such a pivotal role in our lives. How exactly did we reach the point where religious identity has become so superficial and so devoid of deep spiritual significance that we can utter the words "I am a Christian" or "I am a Muslim" and by that mean that our sense of personal identity is completely dependent upon that exclusive claim to religious identification, thereby rejecting as apostasy the competing claims of others? Answering this question will require that we consider the history of the development of the term *religion* and its supposed opposite, *the secular*, as we use these terms in the contemporary language. I will argue that the development of restrictive and exclusive religious identity claims is a direct product of the process of secularization (based on philosopher Charles Taylor's view on the characteristics of secularism), since religion and secularism are locked into a mutually defining relationship such that neither has any real meaning apart from the other. Furthermore, the move toward secularism can itself be understood from a Jungian perspective as the apparent triumph of the human ego.

Understanding what I mean by the triumph of the ego will require an introduction to Jungian psychology. Chapter 3 will therefore be devoted to a summary of Jung's view of human psychological development over the span of a lifetime. Now, I am not as naïve here as I surely seem to be. I am well aware that Freud and Jung have been largely dismissed today by mainstream psychology and psychiatry as anxiety and depression become transformed into medical conditions best treated by a combination of cognitive and behavioral therapy and, increasingly, medication. But I will argue that the medicalization of human emotional suffering so prominently marketed today by the health care industry is itself a symptom of a secularizing tendency that narrows our vision and cuts us off from spiritual depth, thus creating the conditions for an epidemic of anxiety and depression. There is mounting evidence that the commonly repeated "chemical imbalance in the brain" explanation for anxiety and depression has no scientific basis and is rather the propaganda of a pharmaceutical industry seeking to open up bigger markets for its ever-increasing variety of psychodynamic drugs. These drugs may actually be exacerbating the mental illnesses they are designed to treat, which stands as just one more way that the forces of secularism (and its mirror image, religiosity) are contributing to rather than allaying anxiety and depression.

Now, my own experience tells me that the human psyche is a lot more than just a bunch of biochemical reactions firing in a material brain, the foundational assumption of many psychologists and psychiatrists today. After all, the turning point in my own journey through major anxiety was connecting with a therapist who respected psychodynamic approaches to emotional suffering—that and discovering the writings of a Jungian analyst. The behaviorists and drug prescribers were of little help. My newfound belief in the value of a Jungian approach, then, leads me to argue that we are living today in a time best characterized as the collective triumph (or apparent triumph) of the human ego. In large measure we have been cut off by secularism from our own psychological depths, from the realm of what Jung called The Self, the mysterious complex of energy standing at the deepest recesses of the psyche that grounds our true nature and identity. While the shallow concerns of the ego may dominate our psychological life for a time, eventually the bill comes due and The Self demands expression. When this happens, the fragile ego cracks and its provisional identities crumble, leading to a crisis of identity that while profoundly painful holds the promise of connection to our true identity. I think we are now experiencing the beginning of the cracking of the collective human ego. There may be hell to pay for this, but also new opportunity on the far side of the pain.

The opportunity is that we begin to connect with our psychic depths, a process that results in transcending our provisional identities—including religious identities—as we begin to view ourselves beyond the confining lenses of those identities. Opening our field of vision goes a long way toward resolving the anxiety that results from a constricted, shallow view of ourselves and our lives and holds the promise of leading to a more just, sustainable, and humane world. But what exactly does it mean to transcend religious identity? In chapter 4 I will lay out a vision for what it might look like to live beyond adherence to an exclusive religious identity. The paradigm I will employ for this will indeed be a surprising one. Despite all the rancor and discord today regarding Islam and Muslims, I will argue that core principles of the Islamic tradition embody to a large degree this vision of a spiritual movement existing beyond the borders of any clearly defined religious identity. This is not to uphold all or even most Muslims in the world today as models of this vision. Not at all! Many Muslims today see Islam as a provisional religious identity just as much as many Christians do with respect to Christianity. Secularism affects us all! But I do want to uphold core teachings of the Islamic tradition as a useful paradigm for what I am getting at. Many Muslims deny religion as an accurate category label for Islam, and I believe this Muslim denial of religion contains within it profound insights from which we in the West have much to learn.

Finally, in chapter 5, I will gather the insights from previous chapters and lay out a vision for what it could mean both personally and communally to transcend religious identity and live a radically open life. Living this way will require removing obstacles to this kind of life—obstacles that come in the form of a materialist worldview that renders it nearly impossible to engage spiritual depth and the difficulty we face moving beyond the provisional identities that keep us locked into narrow, constricted views of ourselves. Fortunately, there are good reasons—some even arising from empirical science itself—to challenge a materialist worldview. Unfortunately, removing the obstacle of adherence to provisional identities may prove more difficult. But I will nevertheless outline reasons why we should consider trying to tame our triumphant egos. If we can overcome these obstacles to living a radically open life, it may be in our power to reshape the institutions of our collective lives toward the creation of a more just and humane world by transcending artificial dichotomies like natural/supernatural, sacred/profane, and church/state, which keep us locked into a disenchanted secular framework. In the end, living a radically open life will require embracing the mystery of the vast, incomprehensible universe that forms the true context of our lives. Embracing this mystery and being willing to submit to the greater wisdom of the cosmic story will ground us in a greatly widened and deepened perspective that transcends the narrowness of religious identity claims, a move consistent with what Jung offers as the solution to anxiety. As we engage a renewed life individually, we will renew our collective lives as well.

A Persian proverb tells us that the night is indispensible if we want to see the stars. Moving through darkness is scary indeed, but it is only in the darkness of night that we come face to face with the vastness of the universe and the mystery and profundity of the human experience. In the bright light of day we cannot see beyond our immediate surroundings, but the setting of the sun opens us to the glory of the universe. Likewise, the painful darkness of anxiety and depression, short of being medical conditions to be cured, may actually be our invitation to authentic life and an important part of transforming our world, initiating a new era of justice and sustainability. We live in a pain-avoidant and death-denying culture. But to truly live is to feel, and to live fully is to feel deeply. We must stop avoiding our feelings, even if they are painful, and instead allow the pain to guide us through the wilderness and into a place of renewed life. This is not an easy journey, and not necessarily the one we would choose for ourselves. But in a very real sense we have no choice, for the journey chooses us. And this is a good thing too. For it is the journey that truly makes us human, and as such, it is the only journey worthy of our time, energy, and full commitment. Allow me to share a portion of my journey.

one

A Journey through Darkness

MY PROBLEMS BEGAN—OR SO I thought—late in the fall of 2004. One morning I was observing a colleague as he lectured to a class at Luther College when inexplicably a pall of darkness and doom spread over me and I felt as if I were no longer physically present in the classroom. While I was still intellectually engaged in my colleague's lecture, I felt at a deep level as if I were on some strange planet and in some kind of immediate danger with no avenue of escape and no clue what it was I even needed to escape from. Once class was over I returned to my office and busied myself with correspondence, grading of papers, and other routine matters of the life of a college professor, all the while trying to ignore the disturbing feelings with the hope they would resolve as spontaneously as they had begun. No such luck!

Returning home after work, I tried to interact with my wife and children while not letting on how uncomfortable I felt, but to no avail. The feelings of dread and doom were too powerful to hide and I had little choice but to share them with my wife, though there was little help she could offer since I had absolutely no clue what was happening. After a fitful night of sleep, I awoke the next morning to find the demons still smiling at me from the foot of the bed. They followed me wherever I went day after day, week after week, with an unrelenting vagueness that left me powerless to know what to do.

Though I continued to function relatively normally during the day, nights were another matter entirely. Without the busyness of daytime activity to distract me, in the darkness and quiet of my bedroom, the demons had free rein to overwhelm me, rendering sleep difficult at best and impossible at worst. It was finally the mounting sleep deprivation that drove me to the doctor's office, desperate for relief. My doctor ran a battery of tests to make sure nothing was physically wrong, gave me a prescription for the tranquilizer Xanax to help with sleep, and warned me to use it sparingly because of its highly addictive potential. He also informed me that there are physical conditions that can cause feelings of anxiety, some of them quite serious, like liver disease (something else to worry about!).

As I awaited the results of the tests, I experienced firsthand one of the most perverse aspects of anxiety: it makes you hope there *is* something physically wrong with you! I actually found myself rooting for the blood tests to return positive for some type of physical illness, even a serious one. At least then I would know what was wrong; I could (hopefully) be treated, and the disturbing feelings would go away for good. I was terrified that if the tests were negative and no reason could be discerned for my symptoms, I would never live another day without having to battle an overwhelming sense of dread and doom that profoundly darkened every aspect of my daily experience. Not surprisingly, the tests came back negative. I was fit as a fiddle. Just dealing with a bit of stress, according to my doctor. Negative medical tests normally bring a wonderful sense of relief, but for me this news was nothing short of devastating. Now what do I do?

The Xanax did help some with sleep, but fearing addiction I used it quite sparingly, and it was becoming harder and harder to labor through each day utterly clueless about the cause of my predicament and therefore just as clueless about where to turn for help. After many weeks of torment, I finally broke down at the urging of family and friends and made an appointment with a psychologist. I was desperate for relief and could see no other choice. I obviously needed help. But the psychologist was not as desperate to see me—I couldn't get an appointment for another four weeks! Interestingly, between the time I made the appointment and the time I was walking into his office for the first session, I had begun to unravel the mystery on my own.

Coming to Terms with the Past

I was in my mid-forties when this descent into darkness began, not an unusual age for a midlife crisis. But I had earlier struggled with anxiety in my late-twenties—though not as severely—and I began to wonder if there might be a connection between these two episodes. I asked myself, what was the cause of my anxiety then, and could it help explain what was happening now? As it turns out these two episodes of anxiety were very much related, and the connection between them proved so obvious that I couldn't believe I hadn't hit upon it earlier. Not surprisingly, my anxiety was deeply rooted in my formative years as I suspect is the case for many people who struggle emotionally. Unraveling the mystery would require reassessing my life story from the more mature perspective of midlife. What was it about my formative years that was causing me so much trouble now?

Thankfully, I have many happy memories of my childhood. I recall with fondness carefree summers playing sports and other games with my friends, attending family gatherings, and playing chess with my Great Uncle Fred, who always seemed more interested in engaging with me than with other adults. Yet despite these positive memories, I have become acutely aware in more recent years that, happy memories notwithstanding, I am actually the product of a rather dysfunctional family system (who isn't, I suppose?!). Growing up, I tended to be a shy, cautious child, someone lacking a strong sense of independent identity with little interest in asserting myself. My mother, unfortunately, took on the role of the proverbially overprotective parent, sheltering me from the vagaries of the outside world and doing little to encourage my independence. My sister (four years older) was more adventurous and more willing to assert her independence, which put her in a much more adversarial role with our parents and especially our mother. My father held an MBA from the Wharton School of the University of Pennsylvania, the educational credential of many Fortune 500 CEOs. You might expect, then, that we lived a very comfortable upper-middle-class or even upper-class existence. But nothing could be further from the truth. Despite my father's impressive educational accomplishments, he never rose above the level of a midlevel accounting clerk, and his embarrassment at what he saw as professional failure caused him to withdraw from social relationships, rendering him largely emotionally unavailable to the rest of the family. He slaved away each day at a routine job in the payroll department of his company, earning enough to pay the bills and maintain a lower-middle-class existence, but that was about all. He had no hobbies, no close friends, and little inclination to take me under his wing and be a real father.

As tensions between my parents mounted (my mother craved more interaction with other couples), my sister got married, which allowed her to partially escape the rapidly deteriorating family dynamics. With little emotional support from my father, my mother turned to me—her shy, cautious child—for connection, and our emotional bond grew deeper and deeper. At a time when I should have been spreading my wings and asserting my independence, I was instead becoming increasingly absorbed into my mother's overprotective shell. Finally, everything came to a head when, during my junior year in high school, my father was forced to take early retirement as his company downsized (he was too young to collect Social Security), and then his aged parents both died within a week of each other. My father fell into a deep, nearly suicidal, depression and had to be hospitalized. With my sister married and out of the house, it was just me and Mom at home, and fearing being abandoned herself, my mother had no intention at this point of encouraging *my* independence. Fortunately— almost miraculously—my father recovered from his emotional breakdown and returned home in a much better state. But the cards of my own emotional life had already been dealt. By this time I had completely internalized at a deep and largely unconscious level that my mother was my protector. Lacking any strong sense of my own identity, I was convinced I could never live physically or emotionally apart from her. My identity was entirely bound up in hers.

My father's two-month hospitalization in the psychiatric ward of the Veteran's Administration hospital in Philadelphia (he had served in World War II) occurred during the fall of my senior year in high school. At a time when I should have been making college plans, I had little idea what I wanted to do with my life, and the thought of going away from home to attend college absolutely terrified me—unless, of course, I could bring my mother along! But it was all a moot point. There was no money to send me to a fancy out-of-state college, so I applied to Temple University. I could get loans to pay the low in-state tuition, and I could live at home and be a commuter student. Perfect! But what to study? I was good at math, science, and mechanical drawing in high school but avoided subjects like English and history. So at a relative's suggestion, I took up civil engineering. It combined my abilities in math and science, yet was practical enough to perhaps get me a decent job. I enjoyed my college years and did well academically, graduating *magna cum laude*, but I had the misfortune (or was it good fortune?) of graduating in 1982 into the teeth of a major economic recession. Technology jobs were scarce. So with limited options before me, I put very little effort into finding a good engineering job and instead latched onto a dead-end job at a hospital close to home. Oh, and did I mention? This hospital just happened to be my mother's place of employment!

I spent my early and mid-twenties happily living at home, working at my dead-end hospital job and hanging out with friends, while showing little inclination to seek employment more consistent with my educational achievements. (Sound familiar? I was my father's son!) But then things began to change. I met a girl, fell in love, and got engaged. While this was initially a very happy time, six months before the wedding, my first bout with anxiety began. Like the more recent episode, this one also began as a sudden, inexplicable, vague sense of doom and gloom. It is not hard to see in hindsight why this was happening. But at the time I was utterly clueless. I should have been happy, but deep down I knew that getting married meant finally moving out on my own, away from my mother, the one thing I had convinced myself I was incapable of doing. Who wouldn't develop anxiety facing the thing they are most afraid of? With help and support, I managed the anxiety, got married, and got out on my own. And before I knew it, I was quitting my dead-end job to attend seminary, which led to a graduate program in religious studies back at Temple University where I earned my PhD. Things could not have been going better, and I truly believed I had finally developed a sense of independence and personhood that would allow me to stand on my own with confidence, apart from my mother. The demons and dysfunction of my childhood were finally a thing of the past. Following graduate school, I secured a faculty position at Luther College in Decorah, Iowa, and there I continue today.

Anxiety 2.0

Now we return to my mid-forties and the second episode of anxiety. As I headed for my first therapy session, I was convinced that this new round of anxiety must be linked to what I had experienced in my twenties. Yet I had been living in Iowa for almost four years, loved my job teaching in a liberal arts college, and was now raising two wonderful children (one of whom we had traveled to China to adopt—the experience of a lifetime). Clearly, I had finally differentiated myself from my mother and was my own person. Or was I? In December 2001, not quite a year and a half after moving to Iowa, my mother died (my father had died in 1996). Though I was sad about my mother's passing, my life went on pretty much unchanged for the next three years. But this new round of doom and gloom was descending upon me as I approached the third anniversary of her death. It began to dawn on me that I might not have differentiated myself from her as much as I thought. I was now facing the final, inalterable separation from my mother, and I became acutely aware of how truly alone in the world I felt without parents, especially my mother, and how little sense of my own identity I could muster. It felt as if the very sense of myself as a person had gone to the grave with my mother, and the prospect of having to live the rest of my life without her caused sheer terror.

Finally, the four weeks passed and I headed for my first therapy appointment, during which I related my history and my insights about it to my new therapist. I told him I was undergoing a profound identity crisis brought on by a delayed grief reaction to my mother's death. I'm not sure how kindly he took to a new client providing such a detailed self-diagnosis in a preliminary therapy session. Diagnosing my problem, after all, was his job. Not surprisingly, he was not overly impressed with my analysis. He informed me that things like identity crises and midlife crises were not DSM categories and that my problem needed to fit some standard mental health category in order for my insurance to help pay for the therapy.[1] Besides, he thought I knew very well who I was, though he did admit to being somewhat perplexed by my symptoms. His approach to mental health was what is called these days behavioral medicine, meaning his primary goal was to try to reduce the severity of my symptoms and help me feel better. It quickly became apparent that he had little interest in helping me explore the deeper meaning of my mother's death and the profound identity questions it had raised for me, though this latter approach seemed to me like it would have been more helpful. I did not simply want to *feel* better; I wanted to *be* better. Though rather perplexed by my situation, my therapist did admit to having a real professional curiosity about it and had a professional interest in working with me to try to sort it out. Great! I was going to be his research project. This all felt a bit patronizing, but I shouldn't be too hard on him. I really did like my therapist as a person. It's just that he was working from a particular philosophical perspective about the causes of mental illness, a perspective that I do not share and that I will critique as a significant part of the argument of this book.

After a number of sessions, when it became clear that he did not have the answers I was seeking, I ended the relationship and continued to go it

---

1. DSM stands for Diagnostic and Statistical Manual of Mental Disorders, the mental health field's Bible for diagnosing mental illnesses.

alone for awhile. I was convinced I knew what the problem was even though I did not know in any concrete way how to solve it (short of resurrecting my mother!). The entire emotional terrain of my life had been permanently altered by her death, and I had no clue how to live within this new reality, being without any strong sense of an independent identity of my own. Not surprisingly, over the next several months, as I allowed myself to open up fully to the significance of my mother's death, I spiraled down into a deep, dark pit of anxiety and depression that nearly disabled me (following in my father's footsteps again!).

I developed an acute case of agoraphobia, leaving the house only to walk to campus to teach my classes, and even then I frequently developed acute anxiety attacks while standing in front of the class (how I ever kept it hidden from the students, I'll never know!). At home I fell into repeated bouts of intense crying that scared my wife and young children. Twice I registered to attend a scholarly conference in another city only to back out at the last minute, terrified to venture beyond the boundaries of my home and the Luther College campus. One summer, our family drove east toward Pennsylvania to attend a long-anticipated family reunion (anticipated, that is, by my wife since the reunion was with her family!). We drove as far as Rockford, Illinois, where we stopped for the night, but my anxiety became so acute during that night that I was unable to continue the trip and we were forced to turn back and miss the reunion. My life and the lives of those around me became increasingly dictated by my deteriorating emotional state.

Anxiety is often described by mental health professionals as a generalized sense of fear or dread that is not attached to any particular event that would be expected to generate a fear response (like being attacked by a lion). Depression is often described as a feeling of sadness and a loss of interest in pleasurable activities that occurs on most days for at least two weeks. But as anyone who has suffered from major anxiety or depression knows, describing these conditions as feelings of fear and sadness is like calling the Mona Lisa just another painting. There is nothing in the normal range of human emotional experience that is at all analogous to the subjective experience of a major anxiety disorder. I cannot adequately describe what I was feeling because there simply are no words to describe it. Our language is tied to our normal range of experience, so we literally do not have the language to accurately describe such a heterogeneous experience in a way that someone who has not shared it can fully understand. The well-known writer and education guru Parker Palmer has written that he finds his own struggles with depression "difficult to speak about because the experience is so unspeakable."[2] So it is with my anxiety. I couldn't believe it was even possible to feel the things that I felt, and it is utterly impossible to describe it adequately in language that can fully convey my subjective experience. But I will nevertheless do my best.

One of the more pernicious aspects of anxiety is that you begin to fear things that have nothing to do with the underlying cause of the anxiety. Your life becomes consumed by fear, and you begin fearing the fear itself. In my case, I developed an obsessive fear of committing suicide. Now, I did not want to commit suicide, mind you, but anxiety made me feel so out of control that I was afraid some impulse would come over me, forcing me to harm myself against my will. This obsession with suicide is not nearly so irrational as it may sound. Many times, people develop anxiety in response to some particular aspect of their lives. They experience feelings of anxiety when they are in the fear-producing situation (like a problem at work, for example), but they can relieve the anxiety at least temporarily by removing themselves from the situation stimulating their anxiety. For me, unfortunately, it was the entire context of my life that was making me anxious. At a deep emotional level, I simply could not bear to be in the world without my mother, but of course the only escape from life is death. There is no third alternative. Predictably, then, I began having impulsive thoughts about trying to escape my anxiety-producing situation—life itself—by committing suicide, even though at a cognitive level I had no interest in ending my life. These impulsive thoughts were truly terrifying, and I became obsessed with the idea that I might do what I did not want to do. I came to fear being left alone lest I give into a suicidal impulse with no one to stop me. In the evenings, when my wife was upstairs and the children were in bed, I avoided going near the kitchen for fear I would impulsively pick up a knife and slit my wrists. I even got an odd physical sensation on my wrists when I would fantasize about this. Even loading the dishwasher after dinner became a very difficult chore because I was so obsessively afraid to handle knives.

I could go on, but you get the picture. I was in pretty bad shape. Because of the severity of my symptoms, my primary care physician prescribed an antidepressant medication (one of the highly touted selective serotonin reuptake inhibitors [SSRIs] that help with anxiety too). But I did a little research and learned that in some cases, these medications can

2. Palmer, *Let Your Life Speak*, 57.

increase suicidal thoughts, especially at the beginning of treatment or when the dosage is increased. That was the last thing I needed to hear. Already obsessively afraid of committing suicide, I found myself taking a medication that could potentially make me suicidal and force me to do what I did not want to do, which only increased my anxiety further, making it impossible for me to stay on the medication for more than a couple of weeks (and they can take four to six weeks to work). Over time I experimented with three different SSRIs but never took them for more than two weeks at a time because my anxiety drove me off of them; I feared they would cause me to lose the only sense of control I maintained. Anxiety, ironically, prevented me from taking medication for anxiety! But this may have been a profound blessing as we will learn in a later chapter. Antianxiety and antidepressant medications turn out not to be the wonder drugs that the pharmaceutical industry would like you to believe they are.

With my life dangerously close to spiraling out of control, I sought the help of another therapist. My first therapist, who seemed quite clueless about the cause of my symptoms, possessed a PhD in counseling psychology; this new therapist had only a master's degree in social work, so I was not terribly optimistic that she would prove very helpful. Yet after I laid out my history in detail during our first session, she explained that the severity of my symptoms was completely understandable. What a revelation! She was the first person who had truly validated my feelings and helped me see that I was not going crazy. *My suffering made sense and could be understood as an invitation to growth; it was not a disease needing to be cured.* On the one hand, this was great news, but unfortunately it came with a dose of reality too: she really couldn't "cure" my problem since I was not really ill. I was, according to her, on a profoundly personal journey to discover my true identity, an identity that could allow me to stand finally as my own person, apart from my mother. She could support me along the way, but I had to do the hard work of walking through the valley and finding my own way to the light. And she warned that it might not be a short process. I needed to redraw a completely new emotional map for my life.

Given the incredible pain I was in, her words were not easy to hear, but time and hindsight have proven her absolutely right. This book is part of the journey of self-discovery, a journey that has brought me through the proverbial shadow of death and back into a meaningful life. Another important guide through the darkness has been James Hollis, a Jungian analyst who has written a series of books about the miseries of midlife. His

Jungian insights have resonated powerfully with my own experience as I will share in detail in chapter 3. For now, however, I will reconsider the seeming paradox at the center of this book from the perspective of my involuntary experiential education at Anxiety State University. Why is there so much anxiety in such an overtly religious society?

Anxiety and Religious Identity

How exactly do exclusive claims to religious identity help foster the anxiety epidemic? It will require the next few chapters to fully understand this. For now I will simply outline an answer and provide a very brief introduction to Jungian psychology, since it was the very Jungian insights that helped me through my anxiety that also gave me a new perspective on the issue of religious identity. A more thorough treatment of Jungian psychology and its importance for understanding religious identity will form the basis of chapter 3.

Until I was plunged into the depths of anxiety and depression, I had no idea just how much my sense of personal identity had been completely bound up in external relationships with my mother and other primary relatives. Even though I was in my mid-forties and outwardly successful, I had no idea that at a deep emotional level I was clueless as to who I truly was. Lacking a deep connection to myself, I *was* in the throes of a full-blown identity crisis, the protestations of my first therapist notwithstanding. I had been living my entire life according to a set of what Jung might label provisional identities—identities derived primarily from my childhood relationships, not from my own deepest commitments. Now, however, the dynamics of my life had rendered those provisional identities useless, leaving me in a terrifying void. Of course, this is not unique to me. We all develop these provisional identities in our childhood—Jung called them projections. Because we generally are not *consciously* aware of our projections, they tend to exert a powerfully *unconscious* influence on our lives, as my story well attests. For example, I had found ways to completely rationalize the personally limiting decision to live at home during college and to take a job at the hospital where my mother worked following graduation. At the time I would have vehemently denied that I was driven to these decisions by deep emotional needs. Projections by their nature are enormously powerful because they are largely unconscious. Hence they exercise enormous influence over our lives without our even realizing what is happening.

It was only when my mother's death permanently altered the emotional terrain of my life and I was thrown into the abyss of anxiety and depression that I was able to become conscious of what had remained unconscious for so many years. Don't miss the fact that I was able to deny the significance of this enormous change for three years; my mother died in 2001, but it was not until 2004 that the buried emotions forced their way to the surface—and only then much against my will. For awhile I was quite amazed at my ability to remain in denial for so long, but after further reflection it began to make sense. Though I was not consciously aware of it, I knew at a deep unconscious level that there would be hell to pay for opening up to the significance of my mother's death. Of course, I tried to do everything I could to avoid it. It isn't really true that my mother's death had little effect on me for three years. I only *thought* at the time that it hadn't deeply affected me. How wrong I was.

My deep and abiding—but also unconscious—belief that I could not face life on my own apart from my mother truly did dominate my life well into adulthood. I haven't mentioned that after getting married, my wife and I settled into an apartment less than a mile from my parent's house. And when my father died in 1996, my wife and I, at the invitation of my mother, moved back in with her while I finished graduate school. Of course, we rationalized this decision with such arguments as "It will save us money while I finish school," or "I will be spending so much time at my mother's house helping to take care of her anyway, we might as well just move in." These arguments certainly had some truth to them, but were they the real reasons for my dragging my wife back to my childhood home? Why could I not move beyond this provisional identity?

Projections truly dominate our lives and our decision-making. The mere thought of discarding them can be terrifying. This is an important insight. Provisional identities often act as anxiety-management systems. This is one reason why people often perpetuate dysfunctional behaviors. No matter how much trouble a certain behavior causes us, continuing to act in accordance with a provisional identity (or projection) protects us to some degree from the anxiety and depression that would attend its loss. Better to stay with the known than to risk the unknown. At least I know who I am within the confines of a provisional identity. If I move outside, I risk losing all sense of myself, and loss of identity, I dare to venture, is one of the most frightening things that can happen to a person. It is well documented that women often remain in abusive relationships far too long both for fear of the unknown and because their own identities become so distorted by the abuse that they may come to believe they deserve the abuse and cannot see themselves living outside of it.

We all possess anxiety-management systems stemming from our formative years that help us cope with life in a large and fearful world. But beyond these more personal provisional identities, I think we are also witnessing the development of a host of socially induced collective provisional identities, possibly as a way to cope with the rising levels of anxiety attendant to life in the modern world with its superficial concerns and loss of deep spiritual connection. These can come in many forms. There are political identities, nationalistic identities, class identities, and the primary theme of this book—religious identities. Let me comment further on some of these social identity structures.

As I write this book, America's public discourse is becoming increasingly marked by a strong sense of hyper-nationalism. Some politicians are trying to make sharp distinctions between "real Americans" and those who really don't fit the mold. President Obama's status as an American citizen, and thus his legitimacy as president, is being strongly challenged despite a complete lack of evidence. Muslims, even those born in this country, are being vilified as un-American, and President Obama is being counted among them. For these hyper-nationalists, being American has become synonymous with being of white European ancestry (even the only true Americans—Native Americans—are seen as outsiders!), and a powerful sense of identity is derived from this particular ethnic marker. But America is undergoing a seismic demographic shift. As Hispanic, Asian, and other immigrant populations grow, it is certain that by the middle of this century, the portion of the population representing a white European ethnicity will decline to under 50 percent. Nothing symbolizes this demographic shift more concretely than the election of an interracial president with a foreign-sounding name. But this demographic shift will cause considerable anxiety for those whose sense of personal identity is tightly connected to a white European nationalistic identity. So the hyper-nationalistic rhetoric we hear should be read as an anxiety-management system—that is, as a way to reinforce this nationalistic provisional identity to allay the anxiety that would attend discarding this identity and opening up fully to a multicultural future. Of course, the prime example of the use of hyper-nationalism to allay anxiety is probably Nazi Germany. I am sure there was great comfort for many people facing considerable political and economic turmoil to know that they were part of a superior Aryan race. For many Germans, the need to manage anxiety trumped the horrendous evil done in the name of the hyper-nationalist system. Anxiety avoidance is one of the most powerful of all human emotional responses and probably helps explain how so many people could stand idly by in the face of such an atrocity as the Holocaust.

Many people today link their sense of identity and worth to the attainment of material wealth. Economic class identity becomes a powerful anxiety-management system. How do we know this? Just look at what happens to wealthy people when the wealth disappears. How many Wall Street tycoons jumped to their deaths after the stock market crash in 1929? More recently, there were several stories about wealthy businessmen who committed suicide after the economic meltdown of 2008 reduced their net worth by half (from $1 billion to $500 million!). When one's provisional identity is linked to economic class status, failure to continue to accumulate greater sums of wealth can cause considerable anxiety, and when a substantial amount of that wealth disappears—especially when it disappears quickly—the resultant emotional suffering can be too much to bear. The psychodynamics of our modern obsession with wealth accumulation is an area greatly in need of study. But that is another book.

My concern in this book is religious identity, which I think is beginning to function in contemporary America in a manner similar to these political, class, and nationalistic identities—as an anxiety-management system. But religious identity turns out to be a terribly ineffective anxiety-management system because by its very nature it cuts us off from the deep spiritual resources we so desperately need to expand our horizons and overcome the anxiety of modern living. Exactly why this is so will become more obvious in the next chapter. For now I will simply observe that as our lives in the secular world become ever more superficial, and we become cut off from connection to deep spiritual resources, we turn to rather empty affirmations of religious identity and membership in exclusive religious communities to try to allay some of the anxiety that is produced by our disconnection from spiritual depth.

For far too many people today, it doesn't seem to matter too much whether their lives are really informed by the dictates of their religious tradition so long as they can "talk the talk" and wear a particular religious identity label as an identification tag. How else to account for the striking number of high-profile evangelical Christians in recent years who took a firm stand in defense of traditional marriage and family values but turned out themselves to be either adulterers or gay? (Consider also that staunch, pious Muslim Osama bin Laden, whose compound in Pakistan was apparently filled with pornographic material). This hypocrisy stems from wearing the label "Evangelical Christian" (or Muslim) as an identification tag, allowing one to belong to a group of like-minded people. There is safety in numbers. To allay anxiety, membership in an exclusive religious community must be maintained at all cost even if the theological and moral dictates of this community are totally antithetical to one's own deepest commitments. Jung observed that "the Churches stand for traditional and collective convictions which in the case of many of their adherents are no longer based on their own inner experience but on *unreflecting belief*."[3] Unfortunately, we cannot see this when our superficial religiosity severs us from our own psychic depths where our deepest commitments lie. Such adherence to a superficial religious identity might ironically force a gay person (a true identity marker) to adopt a homophobic attitude (a provisional identity tied to group membership), leading to self-hatred and even more anxiety!

But beyond merely engendering hypocrisy, living from provisional identities is highly problematic on at least two other counts. First, while provisional identities can keep anxiety at bay for a time, they are always vulnerable to dissolving and leaving us in the abyss of major anxiety and depression. I was fine—or so I thought—until my mother died. But that provisional identity was never going to carry me all the way through life. If our identity is bound up in money, money can suddenly disappear. Nationalistic identities can be threatened by demographic shifts, as can religious identities. This is why some conservative Christians are terrified that Muslims will take over America and force everyone to follow shari'a law. These Christians are terrified of having their religious identity threatened because the loss of that exclusively Christian identity would result in real emotional turmoil. Likewise, some Muslims fear having to interact with Christians and Jews.

This last point leads to the second big problem with socially constructed provisional identities: they almost always authorize division, prejudice, and, far too often, violence. The 9/11 terrorists who wore the label "Muslim" as an identity tag (their actions prove that they had lost

3. Jung, *Undiscovered Self*, 37; emphasis Jung's.

all connection to the deep spiritual resources of the Muslim tradition) wreaked terrible violence on those they deemed non-Muslim. In reaction, those wearing the label "Christian" engage in acts of overt Islamophobia. The hyper-nationalism of Nazi Germany spelled death for six million Jews. Those whose identity was bound up with the incessant attainment of material wealth brought the American (and nearly the global) financial system to its knees in 2008, leading to economic misery for millions of people. The 1994 Rwandan genocide resulted from colonial oppressors forcing the sharp ethnic distinction Hutu/Tutsi on people who were more alike than different. These examples could be multiplied many times over, but the point is clear. Provisional identities don't really solve the problem of anxiety but actually increase the levels of anxiety in the world by authorizing all kinds of societal discord and violence. Living a radically open life in service to one's own deepest commitments will not only help us feel better individually, but will go a long way toward producing a more peaceful, harmonious, and just world.

How did we get to the point where religious identity has become such a superficial construction, one devoid of any real depth but one that we will, nevertheless, sometimes kill to defend? To answer this we must consider how the process known as secularization has produced religious identity at the same time it has attempted, with varying degrees of success, to disenchant the world and render it devoid of spirit. This is a complicated story, but one we must try to unravel if we are to understand what the common word *religion* really means. For surprisingly it turns out that religion is not the opposite of the secular as many suppose. Religion is itself a product of the secularization process. Religion, it turns out, is the mirror image of the secular, and the implications of this insight are truly profound as we will see in the next chapter.

two

Religious Identity in a Secular World

WHAT IS THE RELATIONSHIP between religion and secularism? Do they stand in opposition to one another as many suppose? It may seem so, but consider the following observation. Overt displays of public religiosity do seem to be on the increase these days, yet, ironically, many Americans would probably describe American society as becoming more and more secular. And there is evidence to justify this impression. Evangelical megachurches may be blooming like dandelions in May, but an increasing number of Americans no longer claim affiliation with any particular religious group. Whereas many years ago, stores were closed on Sunday and churches held Sunday evening prayer services, now Sunday is just another day of the week for an increasing number of people. You can shop, eat out, and attend any number of sporting and entertainment events (traveling youth soccer leagues play havoc with churches' scheduling of Sunday school activities!). Some feel that the United States Supreme Court, through rulings on First Amendment cases, is systematically erasing the public expression of religion and restricting religion to the private sphere, creating a religion-free public square. America is becoming increasingly secular, or so the prevailing theory goes, and some greatly fear this rampant secularism because it seems it may eventually stamp out religion altogether. So how can religiosity and secularism both be on the increase at the same time? Is this even possible? Wouldn't the increase of one automatically lead to the diminution of the other? Not necessarily. Secularism and religiosity, it turns out, may go hand in hand.

To understand this paradoxical relationship, we will need to develop a precise working definition of the term *secularism* since this concept is understood in a variety of ways. The task of defining secularism will occupy us shortly. But first, I want to raise the more fundamental and provocative question of whether religion and secularism really do exist in such an antagonistic relationship that it would be possible for secularism to stamp out religion. Rather than secularism posing an existential threat to religion, could it perhaps be that religion and secularism are actually existentially *dependent* upon one another?

Here is what I mean by existentially dependent. It is nearly impossible to talk about either religion or secularism without in some way referring to the other concept. People generally understand religion as constituting an aspect of human experience that is in some way opposed to secularism, while the secular world is commonly understood as constituting a realm of human experience that is not religious. Now, if these two terms are defined in opposition to one another, a moment's thought will reveal the startling conclusion that neither concept can bear any real meaning *apart* from the other. How could one conceive of a secular world without the existence of a conceptual category called religion that is the very thing that provides the secular world with clear and meaningful boundaries (the secular is that which is not religious)? Consider for a moment the analogous relationship between the terms *light* and *dark*. While we think of them as opposites, they are actually locked into a mutually defining relationship. The concept "light" has no independent meaning apart from the concept "dark" and vice versa. So it is with the concepts "religion" and "secularism." In a very real sense, then, secularism cannot destroy religion without also destroying itself! A religionless world could not be described as secular. Even if it were inhabited by nothing but atheists (assuming, of course, that atheism is not a type of religion), such a world could only be recognized as secular by virtue of the conception of a non-secular (or religious) realm to give meaning to the very idea of the secular.

Perhaps even more startling is the implication that the existence of a secular realm is what renders the concept of religion itself meaningful. We can conceive of the existence of a distinct religious realm only *because* we already have a notion of a secular realm defined in opposition to it. Where there is no religion, there can be no secular, and all that is left is a single integrated reality lacking any need for limiting adjectival modifiers.

This fundamental insight—the mutually defining nature of the concepts "religion" and "the secular"—carries profound implications for how we conceive of religious identity in what many would term a secular world. For if we did not believe that society was becoming increasingly secular, it would be almost by definition impossible to even assert a claim to religious identity since the conceptual category "religion" can only exist in a secular framework. In order to understand, then, how claims to religious identity function in a secular world, we must first grasp this fundamental truth that religious identity claims are only *possible* in a secular world. This may all sound a bit strange and rather abstract, but please stick with me here. Let me try to make this idea more concrete by first tackling the question of what we mean when we use the term *religion*, followed by a discussion of what it means to call the world *secular*. When we have some clarity on how these terms are used, it will reveal some very profound truths about the workings of the human psyche, leading us back to the question of why religious identity claims may actually exacerbate rather than allay epidemic levels of anxiety and depression.

What Is Religion?

What is this thing we call religion? If religion is an entity with a real independent existence in the world, it should be possible to observe it and formulate a precise definition, making it apparent to everyone exactly what religion is. But just try it. As commonly used as it is, the word *religion* has proved notoriously resistant to precise definition. Not that many great thinkers have not tried, mind you. But so far all have failed (the reason will become apparent very soon). But let's give it a try anyway. Even though we are guaranteed to fail, the reason for this failure will reveal important insights.

The word *religion* is clearly a noun, and I suppose we all learned somewhere in grade school that a noun is a part of speech referring to a person, place, thing, or idea. More specifically, nouns function by referring to specific items in the world and distinguishing them from other kinds of things. The noun *chair*, for example, refers to a precisely defined item in the world—a piece of furniture normally equipped with legs and a back on which one sits—and distinguishes it from all other possible items like tables, sofas, and china closets. As soon as an English speaker hears the word *chair*, a very specific image is conjured up in this person's mind, an image that will be shared in its general outline by virtually all other English speakers. There is little controversy over what constitutes a chair. Given the way nouns function, then, we must inquire as to what specific item in the world the noun *religion* refers to. What mental image does this word conjure up? Here is where it gets messy.

The concept religion is really an abstraction; you cannot observe or study it directly. No one walks out the front door and directly observes religion in the way he or she might observe a tree or the sun or the blue-ness of the sky. What someone *can* observe, however, are particular types of religious practice. So you might hear some Christians singing hymns in a church or stumble upon some Buddhist monks meditating and believe that you have thereby observed religion. Or you might observe a Jewish Shabbat service or a Muslim Friday prayer and believe you have observed religion. We can extend this even further. Your attempt to directly observe religion might be enriched by experiencing aspects of Mormonism, Zoro-astrianism, Confucianism, or various kinds of indigenous traditions. How about certain types of American nationalism expressed in American civil religion? Or the capitalist economic system, or professional sports, espe-cially football? What? You don't buy those last two as types of religion? Why not? What is the definition of religion that would include Christianity, Judaism, Islam, Buddhism, Hinduism, and Native American religion but exclude capitalism and professional sports, especially considering that seri-ous scholars of religion have proposed these latter two as valid examples of religious activity? You begin to see the problem. In its popular usage, the category label "religion" becomes stretched so broadly that almost anything can be subsumed under it. When I ask my students to make a list of all the different kinds of religion they can identify, I am consistently amazed at how pliable their notion of religion is. Over and over again they list things like atheism, secular humanism, and the Church of the Flying Spaghetti Monster as types of religion!

The problem here is that if anything can be considered religion, then this unusual noun fails in its primary grammatical purpose to pick out something specific in the world and distinguish it from things that are not religion. If everything in the world is a chair, then the concept "chair" has no meaning. We only understand what the word *chair* means by virtue of its difference from all non-chair items in the world. This is just basic structural linguistics. Likewise, if anything can be religion, then nothing is religion and the word loses any referential value. Clearly, then, popular uses of the word *religion* lack anything even approaching a precise definition. And lacking a precise definition, the term *religion* becomes devoid of meaning. It simply does not refer to any clearly distinct aspect of the world. It is really just an empty category designator into which almost anything can be placed. But this is the popular use of the term. Perhaps scholars can do better.

Indeed, the problem of defining the generic concept religion has exercised some of the greatest thinkers of the last two centuries. The Victorian anthropologist E. B. Tylor thought religion could be defined as belief in animistic spirits. For Emile Durkheim, the father of modern sociology, religion was simply a projection of society itself. Sigmund Freud considered religion a psychological projection of our existential fears, while Karl Marx thought of it as the "opiate of the people." None of these scholarly definitions finds anywhere near universal acceptance, and more problematically, none of them can account for the various kinds of traditions normally considered to be religions (traditions like Christianity, Islam, Judaism, Buddhism, etc.) while simultaneously accounting for the things not normally placed under this category (like politics, economics, science, etc.). More problematic still is the method used by scholars to try to define religion.

Consider Emile Durkheim. Durkheim wrote a seminal volume, *The Elementary Forms of the Religious Life*, in which he went about the process of defining religion by identifying and analyzing all the different kinds of religions as they exist in the world. In Durkheim's words:

> Religion cannot be defined except by the characteristics which are found wherever religion itself is found. In this comparison, then, we shall make use of all the religious systems which we can know, those of the present and those of the past, the most primitive and simple as well as the most recent and refined; for we have neither the right nor the logical means of excluding some and retaining others.[1]

Having studied all these different forms of religion, Durkheim tried to identify their shared elements. Whatever they hold in common must be a feature of the generic concept religion. This procedure sounds logical enough at first glance, but upon further reflection an enormous problem becomes apparent. How can Durkheim identify all the different forms of religion in the world prior to developing a definition of the generic category "religion" that would allow him to make those identifications in the first

1. Durkheim, *Elementary Forms*, 38.

place?! How does Durkheim *know* what the different types of religions are if he does not first know what *religion* itself is?

This kind of circularity plagues virtually all attempts to define religion. Since religion cannot be observed directly, scholars try to get at it through an analysis of the different forms of religion. But this suggests that the common list of religions most people take for granted has come about through an entirely arbitrary process. Things like Christianity, Judaism, Islam, Buddhism, and Hinduism became defined as religions prior to there being any standard definition of the generic concept religion. Now, the process whereby these and other traditions became categorized as religions is a long and complicated one that cannot occupy us in detail here. This history has been much studied and well chronicled.[2] For our purposes, what is important about this history is the mounting evidence demonstrating that the generic concept "religion," understood as a distinct realm of experience clearly distinguishable from a nonreligious (or secular) realm, was in fact invented by Christians in the West, and that the tendency to impose the category religion on the traditions of other people has been a fundamental aspect of Western colonial domination over non-Western peoples and places.

For example, David Chidester's book *Savage Systems: Colonialism and Comparative Religion in Southern Africa* documents in disturbing detail how the scholarly discipline of comparative religion was wielded by Europeans as a strategic instrument in the colonial subjugation of southern Africans in the eighteenth and nineteenth centuries. Comparative religion is the exercise I have been describing here of scholars arbitrarily defining certain cultural traditions as types of religion and then comparing them to one another to see what they share in common and where they differ. It is the complete lack of clarity on what constitutes religion that made this process dangerous in the hands of colonial oppressors.

According to Chidester, during the period of European colonial ventures in southern Africa, comparative religion scholars set about trying to discover what kind of religion the people of southern Africa practiced. They assumed that all people everywhere practiced some form of religion and that being religious was a defining feature of humanity. Working with a definition of religion based on their own Protestant Christian notions, however, these scholars were unable to identify anything among the indigenous

---

2. There are many books dealing with this topic. Two good introductions are Fitzgerald, *The Ideology of Religious Studies*; and Masuzawa, *The Invention of World Religions*.

populations of southern Africa that fit their definition of religion, leading them to the startling conclusion that these people in fact possessed no religion. Of course, if religion was a defining feature of humanity, this denial of religion authorized the conclusion that Africans were not fully human, a conclusion that in turn legitimized their subjugation by European colonial powers.

Chidester shows that once the Europeans had gained some control over the indigenous populations, their analysis of indigenous religion gained in sophistication, and they revised their conclusions to afford a type of religion to the people of southern Africa. This religion was considered to be primitive, however, and was labeled superstition, which compared negatively to the lofty, sophisticated Christianity of the colonialists, further legitimizing colonial oppression. By constructing the people of southern Africa as superstitious children, the colonialists were able to justify denying African claims to land and political autonomy. The superstitious Africans desperately needed the light of civilization brought to them by the Europeans.

Over time, rebellions broke out against colonial oppression, and whenever the Europeans were in danger of losing control, Chidester shows that the comparative religion scholars reverted back to their previous denial of religion in order to justify heavy-handed measures to regain control. Once the rebellions were tamed, the people of southern Africa magically regained their religion! In reviewing this history, Chidester comments on how "definitions of religion have been produced and deployed, tested and contested, in local struggles over power and position in the world. In such power struggles, the term *religion* has been defined and redefined as a strategic instrument."[3]

What is important about Chidester's analysis is the observation that religion *could* be defined and redefined over and over again in the colonial context precisely *because* it lacks any clear or agreed upon definition. The categorization or denial of various cultural traditions as religions is a completely arbitrary process, one that is often bound up in complex political struggles. While it might be the case that religion is often thought to be different from politics, the process of deciding what counts as religion is often done for highly political purposes. In fact, the generic concept religion itself *is* a profoundly political notion!

3. Chidester, *Savage Systems*, 254.

How is this again? Isn't it obvious that religion and politics constitute two separate spheres of human activity such that it makes complete sense to talk about their entanglement or separation? Doesn't the United States Constitution enshrine the separation of the religious and political realms with its First Amendment provisions forbidding state establishment of religion while simultaneously allowing for its free exercise? Not so fast. The religion clauses of the First Amendment assume the ability of the state to precisely define religion. The state must know exactly what the Constitution forbids the state from establishing and what the state must protect the free exercise of. But we have already seen that no such precise definition of religion exists, rendering the religion clauses of the First Amendment incoherent and the highly touted American ideal of religious freedom impossible to attain.

This is the conclusion, at least, of Winnifred Sullivan in her book *The Impossibility of Religious Freedom*. Sullivan considers a 1998 court case, *Warner v. Boca Raton*, wherein a group of Protestants, Catholics, and Jews filed suit against the city of Boca Raton, Florida, for infringing on their First Amendment rights for the free exercise of religion. The issue was this: The city of Boca Raton operated a nonsectarian cemetery and passed an ordinance making it illegal to decorate graves with any kind of upright statues, crosses, or Stars of David. Only flat memorial plaques were allowed in the cemetery to make it easier for groundskeepers to cut the grass and maintain the property. The claimants argued that decorating the graves with upright markings was religiously meaningful to them and charged that this ordinance violated their constitutional rights to the free exercise of their faith. The judge, therefore, was put in the awkward position of having to determine whether this practice of marking graves in a particular manner constituted religion or not. In the end he decided it did not and upheld the city's ordinance.

But think about the significance of that last sentence. In the end *he, the judge,* decided what did and did not count as religion in order to determine if the free exercise clause of the First Amendment applied. Because there is no clear and precise definition of religion, the judge—an agent of the secular state—enjoys the privilege of defining and redefining religion anew in each and every First Amendment case. Of course, judges will often look to previous cases for precedents, so it is not as if they are just making up a new definition of religion from scratch every time. But it is still the case that religion is being defined by an agent of the state despite the constitutional prohibition against state establishment of religion! This leads Sullivan to conclude, "'Religion' can no longer be coherently defined for the purposes of American law."[4] So the cat is out of the bag. The idea of separation of church and state so strenuously defended by so many people in this society—both religious and secular—is really an American myth. David Sehat even calls it this in his excellent book *The Myth of American Religious Freedom*, in which he tells the story of state-sanctioned religious and moral coercion throughout American history. The separation of church and state does not exist; we merely talk as if it does. And herein lies the key to defining what this strange thing called religion really is.

There is no specific item or realm in the world called religion that possesses an independent existence clearly distinct from things that are not religion, like politics and economics. Religion exists only as a way of talking about the world, and this way of talking about the world is a modern Western anomaly. Throughout most of history, most people throughout the world did not view the world as possessing a distinctly religious realm separate from a nonreligious one. Native Americans today do not view the world as consisting of distinct sacred and secular realms, nor do indigenous cultures around the world or the majority of people in Asia. And it is clear that religion did not exist as a clear conceptual category in the worldviews of ancient peoples either. There is no word for religion in biblical Hebrew or Greek, nor is there one in Arabic. This will be a somewhat jarring idea for modern Western people, for it implies that the contemporaries of figures like Jesus and Muhammad could not almost by definition have understood them as primarily religious figures. It is this fundamental idea that formed the basis of my previous book, *Was Jesus a Muslim? Questioning Categories in the Study of Religion*, and I point the reader there for a more thorough discussion of the implications of this idea for Christian-Muslim relations in the contemporary world.

Here in the modern West, however, we do talk about the world as if it possessed a distinct conceptual category called religion that we can clearly distinguish from a nonreligious realm we term the secular. While ancient and non-Western peoples tend to view the world as an integrated whole, it is uniquely in the modern West that we conceptually and linguistically impose on this otherwise unified reality a conceptual dualism: the sacred and the profane. We talk about the world as if there really exists a distinct sacred realm radically opposed to the profane realm of our ordinary experience.

4. Sullivan, *Impossibility of Religious Freedom*, 150.

Religion then becomes the entity through which we interact with this sacred realm—the realm of God, or the gods, or the transcendent—while political, economic, and social structures and institutions come to define the secular realm. But serious and thoughtful people will place certain aspects of the so-called secular realm, like nationalism, capitalist economics, or sports, in the category called religion, rendering the boundary between the sacred and the profane a constantly shifting arbitrary border that exists only in our conceptual imagination; it has no real existence in the world. If it did, we could observe it and formulate a precise definition. But we can't precisely because religion exists only as part of the modern Western dualistic worldview.

Thus, the twin concepts "religion" and "the secular" actually come into existence together. Neither can exist without the other. One can only talk about a secular world to the extent that one conceives of a religious realm that can be put in opposition to it. Absent the concept of religion, it would be meaningless to describe any aspect of the world as secular. There would not *be* a secular world; there would just be a world, an integrated reality lacking any qualifying adjectives. This is a crucial insight for the matter of religious identity. As we saw earlier, religious identity can only *exist* in a secular world, rendering religious identity labels simply by-products of our modern Western sacred/profane dualistic worldview. Religious identity is simply a product of how we talk about the world; it has no meaningful existence in and of itself. It makes little sense, for example, to say that Moses was Jewish, or Jesus was Jewish or Christian, or that Muhammad was Muslim in the way in which we employ those religious identity markers today. Exclusive claims to religious identity—I am a Christian, I am a Muslim, I am an atheist—only have meaning because we live in a cultural context that makes a conceptual separation between religion and the secular. Where this conceptual separation does not exist, exclusive claims to religious identity, and the very idea of religious identity itself, become impossible! But, of course, we live in a world where people *do* make exclusive claims to religious identity, claims that sometimes lead to violence and war. So to say that religious identity is an artificial construction is not to deny its powerful influence in the world. Discourses are powerful things! So we cannot simply dismiss religious identity claims as having no value. They clearly are doing something really important. But what? Before answering this we must tackle the question of what it means to describe modern Western society as secular.

What Is the Secular?

As we saw earlier, a commonly held notion says that modern Western society is characterized by a high degree of secularism. But what does this actually mean? What distinguishes a secular world from a non-secular one? Few people are better able to help us answer this than philosopher Charles Taylor, who takes up this very question in his eight-hundred-plus-page magnum opus *A Secular Age*. In this work Taylor distinguishes three senses in which Western society could be described as secular—two commonly held notions and a third of his own creation. While it is Taylor's third option that I want to concentrate on here, it will be helpful first to briefly summarize the two more traditionally held notions of secularism.

In the first sense, Taylor describes secularism as being characterized by an attempted separation of political structures from religious institutions, or the idea of separation of church and state. In this view, political and religious institutions have their own autonomous essence, and, to quote Taylor, "in our 'secular' societies, you can engage fully in politics without ever encountering God."[5] According to Taylor, not encountering God in the political arena would have been unthinkable five hundred years ago when it was impossible to engage in any kind of public activity without encountering God. So in this first sense, secularity is understood as the systematic emptying from public spaces of any reference to God or other transcendent reality.

Whether this can count as an adequate definition of secularism is open to debate. Separation of church and state—or public secularity—is deeply enshrined within American sensibilities, and yet America retains one of the highest measures of religious belief and practice among its citizens of any nation in the world. Does the separation of the political and religious realms really constitute secularity if people continue to engage in religious practice in such high numbers? Secularizing public space does not seem to be enough to kill off religion. Rather, it sets clear boundaries for religion, which ironically might help religion flourish. America is religious *because* it is secular. Given the overriding ambiguity in this first sense of secularism, a second option has been offered. In the second sense, secular societies are said to be characterized by a general falling off of religious belief

5. Taylor, *Secular Age*, 1.

and practice. Fewer and fewer people profess belief in God or a spiritual realm, and they stop attending churches and other religious institutions in significant numbers. In this sense, Western Europe is one of the most secularized places in the world. The low percentage of church attendance in Western European countries has been well publicized. Now, while there is little doubt that institutional separation of church and state and/or sharply declining numbers of people engaged in regular religious observance might be characteristics of those societies we would label secular, Taylor offers a third sense that forms the framework of his book and that I will summarize in some detail here. It is this third view of secularism that will prove most instructive for the thesis I am developing—that exclusive claims to religious identity in the West, and particularly in America, may exacerbate our epidemic levels of anxiety rather than allay them.

To get a handle on what it means to characterize the modern age as secular, Taylor turns his focus to what he terms "the conditions of belief." The movement toward greater levels of secularism in society consists, for Taylor, of "a move from a society where belief in God is unchallenged and indeed unproblematic, to one in which it is understood to be one option among others, and frequently not the easiest to embrace."[6] Five hundred years ago in the West, it was impossible, according to Taylor, not to believe in God. God was infused in all aspects of life, and nonbelief simply did not occur to most people as a viable option. And the few who did view nonbelief as a viable option were quickly marginalized as heretics and dealt with rather harshly (like burning them at the stake!). Today, however, belief in God has become a choice that one makes among a number of different options, and nonbelief, or atheism, is a perfectly acceptable option exercised by a significant number of people. (Of course, there are still many people who view atheism negatively, but the right to be an atheist is firmly protected by the state in a way unthinkable five hundred years ago when atheists could be executed!). It is this shift toward the viability of unbelief that Taylor spends over eight hundred pages trying to account for. Certainly I cannot provide a full discussion of such an elaborate work, but it will be helpful to pick up on a couple of the significant threads in Taylor's argument.

Taylor begins with the observation that we all see our lives as having what he calls a certain moral or spiritual shape. He writes, "Somewhere, in some activity, or condition, lies a fullness, a richness; that is, in that place (activity or condition), life is fuller, richer, deeper, more worth-while, more

6. Ibid., 3.

admirable, more what it should be."[7] At some time or other we all probably have experienced this sense of fullness, but Taylor wants to inquire about the location of this sense of fullness. Where do we find it?

First, we need to clarify what Taylor means by the experience of fullness. In this I can do no better than to relate the example Taylor himself gives from the autobiography of Bede Griffiths, a twentieth-century Benedictine monk who lived for many years in India. I will reproduce this example in full here because I think it is likely to resonate with many readers and render this idea of fullness in stark relief. It certainly resonates with me. In his autobiography, Griffiths writes:

> One day during my last term at school I walked out alone in the evening and heard the birds singing in that full chorus of song, which can only be heard at that time of the year at dawn or at sunset. I remember now the shock of surprise with which the sound broke on my ears. It seemed to me that I had never heard the birds singing before and I wondered whether they sang like this all year round and I had never noticed it. As I walked I came upon some hawthorn trees in full bloom and again I thought that I had never seen such a sight or experienced such sweetness before. If I had been brought suddenly among the trees of the Garden of Paradise and heard a choir of angels singing I could not have been more surprised. I came then to where the sun was setting over the playing fields. A lark rose suddenly from the ground beside the tree where I was standing and poured out its song above my head, and then sank still singing to rest. Everything then grew still as the sunset faded and the veil of dusk began to cover the earth. I remember now the feeling of awe which came over me. I felt inclined to kneel on the ground, as though I had been standing in the presence of an angel; and I hardly dared to look on the face of the sky, because it seemed as though it was but a veil before the face of God.[8]

Reflect upon your own experiences for a moment. Think of a time when you experienced that wonderful moment that comes along far too infrequently when you were lifted out of your ordinary sense of being in the world and afforded a glimpse of something larger and more powerful than yourself. An experience that filled you with a sense of awe and wonder and that by comparison renders your normal daily routine rather hollow and meaningless. An experience whereby you might think you have caught

7. Ibid., 5.
8. Quoted in Taylor, *Secular Age*, 5.

a brief glimpse of a transcendent reality. No one can deny the power of these experiences of fullness when everything seems richer, deeper, and more worthwhile, but in Taylor's words, "we have moved from a world in which the place of fullness was understood as unproblematically outside of or 'beyond' human life, to a conflicted age in which this construal is challenged by others who place it (in a wide range of different ways) 'within' human life."[9]

Griffiths spontaneously experienced the singing of the birds and the beauty of the flowers as a glimpse of a transcendent world, an experience that seemed to transport him into the very presence of God. Given that he was a Benedictine monk, I suppose his interpretation is not surprising. But what Taylor finds significant is that more and more frequently today, people are inclined to place the locus of their experiences of fullness entirely within the material human realm. We may still experience these "highs," but we are more inclined to simply pass them off as the mere side effect of biochemical reactions in the brain brought on by certain functions of the human psyche, which itself is increasingly treated as just an epiphenomenon of neural activity. For many people today, these experiences are manifestly *not* considered authentic interactions with a realm beyond the material world; the existence of a transcendent realm is coming to be seen by an increasing number of people as impossible, as nothing more than a superstition left over from a more primitive era of human development. We have moved beyond such childish beliefs, as the story goes.

Taylor argues that by reframing all human experience as deriving entirely from things found within the human realm, we make human material flourishing the highest goal of our existence. No longer do we have a sense that there are goals in life that might go beyond mere human flourishing, like living our lives for the purpose of serving God, or finding the purpose of life in the serving of other people, or just simply living with some sense that our existence has a higher purpose even if we can't articulate exactly what that might be. On the contrary, life becomes self-serving. It is about advancing our own personal goals as far as we can push them, reaching our own potential as human beings. Taylor writes, "a secular age is one in which the eclipse of all goals beyond human flourishing becomes conceivable; or better, it falls within the range of imaginable life for masses of people. This is the crucial link between secularity and a self-sufficing humanism."[10]

9. Ibid., 15.
10. Ibid., 19.

As experiences of fullness become disengaged from the possibility of connection to a transcendent reality, and individual human flourishing becomes the be-all and end-all of life, the world rapidly becomes disenchanted. The physical environment in which our lives are enfolded is seen as nothing more than inanimate matter, just the flow of atoms, molecules, and energy. Living beings themselves come to be understood as nothing more than complex concatenations of matter and energy. The world is no longer alive; it is no longer animated by spiritual beings or transcendent powers. That Native Americans and other indigenous people regularly converse with the spirits of dead family members seems completely silly to modern Western sophisticated folk. For Taylor, this loss of enchantment is a great loss, for it drains meaning and excitement out of daily living, the latter becoming for many people just a boring succession of days marked by the dutiful discharging of responsibilities to family, employer, and society. Not that being responsible to those in our lives is unimportant. It's just that it feels for many people like this is all they do. Life lacks the excitement that comes from taking part in a larger story. We bear life as best we can, but we often fail to fully embrace it.

Life lived in a disenchanted world is captured well by the writer of the book of Ecclesiastes:

> The sun rises and the sun goes down,
>> and hurries to the place where it rises.
> The wind blows to the south,
>> and goes around to the north;
> round and round goes the wind,
>> and on its circuits the wind returns.
> All streams run to the sea,
>> but the sea is not full;
> to the place where the streams flow,
>> there they continue to flow.
> All things are wearisome;
>> more than one can express;
> the eye is not satisfied with seeing,
>> or the ear filled with hearing.
> What has been done is what will be,
>> and what has been done is what will be done;
> there is nothing new under the sun. (1:5–9)[11]

Or in the words of an old song:

11. Quoted from *The Holy Bible: New Revised Standard Version.*

The sun comes up and the sun goes down / the hands on the clock
   keep goin' around
As soon as I get up it's time to lay down / life gets tee-jus, don' it?

I have vivid memories of my father dutifully leaving the house every morning for his accounting clerk job, returning home every evening to eat dinner, read the newspaper, watch television, go to bed, and arise the next morning to repeat the same pattern all over again. This routine was rarely, if ever, broken by engagement in fulfilling hobbies, exploring new things, developing new talents. My father did what he had to do to pay the bills, keep a roof over our heads and food on the table, but he merely endured life; he never fully embraced it. And sadly, he is far from alone in this.

Cut off from any sense of enchantment in our secular age, we naturally try to create it artificially. This is my explanation at least for what might be termed the "Harry Potter phenomenon." No doubt J. K. Rowling is a fantastic writer and storyteller, but we still have to wonder how it is that a series of books originally intended for adolescent readers became an international phenomenon among adult readers and moviegoers. Why are we so infatuated with Harry? I suspect it is because Harry lives in an enchanted world. There are spirits everywhere and every day is an adventure. To be sure, not all of these spirits are benign; many have Harry's utter destruction as their goal. But Harry's whole life is circumscribed by a context larger than himself, an epic struggle between the forces of good and evil. As the only one truly capable of defeating Lord Voldemort, Harry's life bears a meaning far beyond himself. Human flourishing, he learns, cannot be his ultimate goal. The fate of the earth rests in his hands. To make our mundane, disenchanted lives bearable, we retreat into these fantasy worlds of our own creation and vicariously experience the enchantment missing from the real world. We all secretly wish we could be Harry, that our lives could bear a larger significance like his. After all, how cool would it be to be able to fly on a broom and play Quidditch or wizard chess?! Living in a world animated by spirits involved in an epic struggle, while dangerous, is a lot more exciting than cooking, cleaning, paying bills, and just trying to get by. I should confess here that I have not read a single Harry Potter book and have seen only a couple of the movies. While I would never win a Harry Potter trivia contest, that I know the basic outline of the story demonstrates how thoroughly Harry's story has become embedded in our enchantment-starved world.

This longing for an enchanted world is probably also the explanation for the popularity of apocalyptic end-time scenarios within evangelical Christian circles (the world was supposed to end twice in 2011, but we're still here!). It is a lot more exciting to believe that Jesus is going to return imminently and fight an epic battle against Satan than it is to think that our mundane, routinized lives are going to continue on indefinitely until we are annihilated in a scary, mysterious process called death. Now, I realize that fascination with apocalyptic scenarios is not characteristic only of the modern age. Apocalyptic literature like the biblical book of Revelation shows that the apocalyptic imagination was alive and well two thousand years ago, and there is ample evidence for the occasional spike in apocalyptic fervor throughout history (such as around the end of the first millennium). People in these earlier times were not living in the modern, secular, disenchanted world. What accounts, then, for their apocalyptic fervor? In these earlier times, belief in God's imminent and dramatic breaking into the world was fueled by the fact that earthly life was physically difficult. Whether among those living under the weight of Roman imperial oppression who wrote the biblical book of Revelation, or those living through the horrors of Europe's Dark Ages, a period of unrelenting wars, plagues, and serfdom, the apocalyptic imagination served to provide hope for escape from the physical sufferings of earthly life. But such is not the case with modern Western people who enjoy a material standard of living unmatched in history. Apocalyptic fervor is not ignited by a desire to escape from *physical* suffering, but by a desire to escape the *emotional* suffering authorized by the boredom of living in a materially comfortable but spiritually empty world.

There is clearly a strong urge for people to be able to see their lives as participating in some larger story, some larger purpose that goes beyond mere human flourishing. But the ability to connect to such a larger story requires the conviction that such a larger context really exists and that our experiences of fullness actually do represent authentic experiences of connection to something larger and more mysterious than ourselves. Loss of this ability to truly believe in the existence of an enchanted world and the concomitant turning to immanent human flourishing as the primary goal of life is, for Taylor, one of the chief characteristics of our secular age. An enchanted world animated by spirits has been replaced by "a world in which the only locus of thoughts, feelings, spiritual élan is what we call minds; the only minds in the cosmos are those of humans; and minds are bounded, so that these thoughts, feelings, etc., are situated 'within' them."[12]

We should note here that the word *secular* comes from the Latin *saeculum*, which refers to a century or age. In the medieval period, *saeculum* was often put in opposition to spiritual practices in such a way that being in the *saeculum* meant being embedded in ordinary time—unlike monks, for example, who were living in closer connection to eternal time. The word *secular*, then, comes to denote the mundane world of ordinary linear time, and a secular life is one lived as a linear series of days, weeks, years leading to some vague end. It is through enchantment that one connects to higher time, time understood not as a linear series of moments but as an event of overarching significance. When we ask, "What time shall I meet you tomorrow?" we are referring to ordinary secular time. But when we say, "The ambulance arrived just in time to save her life," the word *time* is designating a moment of much larger significance. This distinction between different ways of expressing time is captured by the Greek language with the two words *chronos* and *kairos*; the former denotes linear ordinary time (hence the word *chronological*), whereas the latter denotes the perfect time for something to happen. Given that we so infrequently connect to *kairos*, a sense of higher time, and instead live our lives embedded in a disenchanted world of ordinary chronological time that leads to some vague, unknown end, is it any wonder that secularism breeds anxiety?! But please don't miss the profound implication here. *If secularism breeds anxiety, then religion must as well since we have already established that notions of religion and the secular are inextricably linked and arise into our conceptual world together!*

At this point there is an enormous question staring us squarely in the face. You may have already noticed it, but perhaps not. Consider this: If the shift toward secularity as described by Taylor is in fact characterized by the change from a world where nonbelief in God is nearly unthinkable to a world where belief is just one option among many; from a world in which experiences of fullness were understood as valid experiences of connection to a transcendent realm to one where such experiences are reduced to the material workings of our physical world; from an enchanted world where life takes on an otherworldly significance to a disenchanted one of boring, mundane routines; if this shift brings us to a point of boredom, depression, and anxiety, then why in heaven's name have we allowed it to occur? Are we masochists? Maybe, but the answer is not so simple. For all the apparent

---

12. Taylor, *Secular Age*, 29.

emotional turmoil that life in our secular age authorizes, there is one part of the human psyche that flourishes in a secular environment, a part of the human psyche willing to sacrifice an enchanted, transcendent world in order to fulfill its own self-centered goals. Secularism fuels the triumph of the human ego.

Secularism and the Human Psyche

The final insight I will draw from Charles Taylor is a truly profound one, as it connects deeply to human nature. According to Taylor, the turn to secularism, in addition to the characteristics already considered, also creates a new sense of freedom that would have appeared inconceivable in the past. He writes concerning life in a secular age:

> We feel a new freedom in a world shorn of the sacred, and the limits it set for us, to re-order things as seems best. We take the crucial stance, for faith and glory of God. Acting out of this, we order things for the best. We are not deterred by the older tabus, or supposedly sacred orderings. So we can rationalize the world, expel the mystery from it . . . A great energy is released to re-order affairs in secular time.[13]

Notice how many times Taylor repeats the words *we* and *us* in this passage. Unlike Harry Potter—who lives in an enchanted world of spirits and powers larger than himself, powers that drive the very contours of his life—we live in a secular age freed from the constrictions of such powers. Harry must live in service to these overarching powers. He has no real choice. He must constantly deal with the humbling truth that the fate of the world hinges on his defeat of these powers. But we live now in service only to ourselves, and this idea brings with it an exhilarating freedom. *We* have the power to remake the world in whatever way *we* please. Life revolves around *us* and *our* desires. As the humanistic dictum goes, man (and woman, too!) has truly become the measure of all things.

Taylor pointedly understands this newfound freedom to be a major cause of the rise of humanism. And it is not difficult to see why. Where our lives no longer revolve around activities like appeasing the gods or humbly repenting before God for our sin in hopes of forgiveness and eternal redemption, our lives become our own and our energies are turned toward

13. Ibid., 80.

our own fulfillment as human beings. A certain healthy humility goes out the window and human arrogance takes over. We will decide our own fate, thank you. Though we might still nominally pray for God's assistance in our human affairs, it is clear who is running the show. God is enlisted on the side of our agenda, and critical reflection on the question of whether our agenda is God's agenda is hard to come by. Even professional football players make the absurd claim that God played a role in their winning a big game, totally unaware of how such claims trivialize the very God they profess to be omnipotent and omniscient. After all, as the joke goes, if God was not a Penn State fan, then why did he make the sky blue and white? (I originally wrote this prior to the unfortunate child sex abuse scandal. God's opinion of Penn State may be different today!) Now, I'm sure this was always meant as a joke (at least I think it was, but as one who married into an entire family of Penn State alums, I'm never quite sure!), it does show how far we have come that today God may be more frequently treated as a character in jokes than in any other way. The awe-inspiring reverence for transcendent power likely held by our pre-secular (and therefore pre-religious) ancestors completely dissolves in the face of the drive toward the maximization of human potential (though we must not forget that ego-driven urges to accumulate power have been a constant feature of human civilization).

Using psychoanalytic concepts popularized by Sigmund Feud and Carl Jung, this shift to a secular age can only be described as the triumph of the human ego. I will deal with the Jungian paradigm in more depth in the next chapter. For now it will suffice to note that for Jung, the ego is that part of the human psyche that underwrites the subjective sense of self as a unique individual. Whenever I say "I," it is my ego that is speaking. The function of the ego is to build up a sense of self as an autonomous human being capable of navigating the treacherous territory of life with some measure of competence. This ego identity begins to develop in childhood and continues on into adult life. But it develops based on the interactions we have with parents and siblings in childhood, and later with our spouse or partner, coworkers, and the larger societal structures in which we play a role. For Jung, ego identity does not represent our true identity. The latter is found rather in the Self, a mysterious energy that flows through the deepest recesses of our psyche and connects us to an infinitely expansive transcendent reality. Ego identities are only provisional; they allow us to navigate the world of our sense experience, but they do not define who we truly are.

Though most of us live the majority of our lives within the limits of our ego identity, the Self eventually demands acknowledgment and attempts to break through. This eruption of the Self and its demand to be consciously acknowledged is what often leads to a major crisis of identity. As the Self calls the ego identity into question, the ego fights back and tries to retain control. The effect of this struggle between the ego and the Self will occupy us in the next chapter. Here it is important to point out that an ego identity once firmly developed is not easily discarded. And since it is the ego that centers us on ourselves and our own human potential, the development of a secular landscape creates the perfect conditions for the ego to continue to advance its individualist and self-centered humanistic agenda. The turn toward secularism (at least as defined by Taylor) truly does represent the triumph of a collective human ego.

The problem, according to Jung, is that the ego identity is merely provisional and not representative of our true nature or identity. This would suggest by extension that our collective secular identity as people whose highest goal in life is the maximization of human flourishing is also provisional and therefore not representative of our true collective identity. So in our adherence to a rampant secularism, we are in a sense living a lie. Why don't we give it up then? Because the Self demands more of us than we are normally ready to give. The Self wants to enlarge our vision beyond mere individualistic human flourishing and calls us to a much larger purpose. But this larger purpose is mysterious and uncertain. Our more limited provisional ego identities are safer, so we naturally want to cling tightly to what we know rather than radically open ourselves to the unknown, the uncertain.

Cut off from larger social structures and rituals that would encourage and support us in embarking on the journey inward to the Self, we flounder, clinging tightly to our provisional ego identities and doing our best to minimize the boredom, depression, and anxiety we experience along the way. While our provisional ego identities are multidimensional and include identities acquired from a multiplicity of relationships, I want to argue that the exclusive claim to religious identity has become a very important dimension of this provisional ego identity. If I assert, "I am a Christian," and I mean by this that I am not a Jew, nor a Muslim, nor a Hindu, I am asserting an identity that has meaning only within the context of the secular age that produced all these religious identity labels in the first place. This is the great irony. Since religious identity is the product of a secular framework, it must accept the superficial character of the secular worldview, leading to a kind of functional atheism whereby people may intellectually affirm faith in God while simultaneously living in a way that fails to exhibit any signs of a deep emotional and spiritual connection to transcendent reality. The Native American scholar Vine Deloria once remarked how strange it is that though Christians believe they are going to heaven when they die, they still go to extraordinary lengths to avoid death as long as possible! Just how strong are these convictions about eternal life?!

Struggling to stay afloat in this sea of disenchanted secularism, our egos invent impermeably bounded religious identities in order to buffer us from the dizzying uncertainty contained in the big questions of life. Why are we here? What does it all mean? Who are we? Many important thinkers have wrestled with these questions throughout history and have offered a variety of tentative answers. But what happens today in far too many cases is that religious communities coalesce around a particular set of answers, and rather than participate in the ongoing human process of wrestling with uncertainty and ambiguity, they enshrine their particular answers as invariant truth in the form of religious doctrines to which absolute allegiance is expected. This creates an air of certainty in an uncertain world, which might help allay anxiety for a while. But by completely intellectualizing the pursuit of truth, deep emotional connection to a reality transcending our capacity to comprehend it is sacrificed, leading in many cases to a kind of functional atheism. We say we believe in God, but do we really *feel* divine reality in the gut? In reality, exclusivist claims to religious identity are born out of a need to manage the anxiety of secular disenchantment. It is a classic fear response.

Adhering to an exclusive claim to religious identity shared by other like-minded people may buffer the ego from the larger demands of the Self. But there is a big price to pay. I can hold to an exclusive religious identity only insofar as I live in a secularized world, meaning that I can hold to my exclusive claim to religious identity only as long as I accept the disenchantment that goes along with secularism. Religious identity, rather than fostering spiritual growth and the attainment of spiritual depth, actually does the opposite. By helping me navigate life in a purely materialistic world of disenchantment, religious identity keeps me anchored in a place of superficial spirituality. The development of spiritual depth and maturity requires opening up to the demands of the Self, and the Self cares little about our human-created religious identity labels. This is a scary prospect, especially in a world that does not provide the kinds of social supports that would encourage the exploration of our own emotional and psychic depths. So we take the safer road and cling for dear life to superficial provisional identities.

It is no coincidence that the rise of various forms of religious fundamentalism is a recent phenomenon, not developing in any significant way until the twentieth century. The concept of fundamentalism was not used to describe Christianity until the 1920s in the fundamentalist/modernist controversy that framed the famous Scopes Monkey Trial about the teaching of evolution in the schools. Conservative evangelical Christianity is flourishing in the twenty-first century, as is intolerant fundamentalist Islam. But why now? The rise of exclusivist religious identities parallels the development of secularism and the disenchantment of the world. And it is not just exclusivist religious identities that are reigning in the contemporary world, but also other forms of exclusivist identities expressed in various types of nationalism, racism, and ethnicism. Just look at how popular Samuel Huntingdon's "Clash of Civilizations" theory has become as a way of understanding the future of global politics. He implies that we must engage in battle with those who are not like us! Life in a disenchanted world cuts us off from our own spiritual depths, forcing us to transform provisional identities into claims of absolute identity in order to at least attempt to allay the anxiety that attends disenchantment. The claim "I am a Christian" is transformed from an assertion of one's deep and humble connection to God as revealed in Jesus Christ to an assertion of absolute exclusive identity characterized by intolerance to ambiguity and difference. But this really doesn't work very well. Exclusivist identity claims are born of fear, and fear is the outward expression of the anxiety lurking beneath the surface of our provisional identity constructions. The importance of this connection between exclusivist claims to religious identity and the workings of the human psyche is extremely important and cannot be overstated. Hence, I will devote the entirety of the next chapter to a detailed engagement with a Jungian understanding of human psychological development.

three

Jung and the Failure
of Religious Identity

CARL JUNG MADE THE following observation about the cause of human emotional suffering (what he called neurosis):

> I have frequently seen people become neurotic when they content themselves with inadequate or wrong answers to the questions of life. They seek position, marriage, reputation, outward success or money, and remain unhappy and neurotic even when they have attained what they are seeking. Such people are usually confined within too narrow a spiritual horizon. Their life has not sufficient content, sufficient meaning. If they are enabled to develop into more spacious personalities, the neurosis generally disappears.[1]

If Jung is right, then the etymology of the word *anxiety* (which remember stems from an Indo-European root meaning narrow or constricted) does in fact point to the cause of anxiety. Anxiety results from a narrow and constricted view of our own nature, from a lack of depth and a narrowed spiritual horizon. The cure, then, is to pry open that spiritual horizon, to expand our awareness of our own natures, to develop more spacious personalities. But how do we do so, and where can we turn for help? Many people, I suppose, would turn to religion. Religion is, virtually by definition, that aspect of our experience through which we engage spiritual questions. Religion is where we turn to inquire about the true nature of reality, the meaning of human existence, the meaning of death, and all of life's bigger questions.

---

1. Jung, *Memories, Dreams, Reflections*, 140.

But as we have seen, American society is highly religious, yet at the same time mired in high levels of anxiety and depression. What accounts for this apparent paradox? Why is it that religions have largely failed to effect the enlarging of our spiritual horizons in the way Jung speaks of? Given the discussion in the previous chapter about the characteristics of our secular age, the answer to this dilemma should be fairly obvious. As our society loses touch with the possibility of transcendent connection; as our focus devolves to human flourishing as the ultimate purpose of life; as our worldview narrows down to one that tries to explain all phenomena as resulting simply from interactions between inanimate matter and energy; as the world becomes disenchanted and we find ourselves fully absorbed into the demands of ordinary linear time, spirituality gets pushed to the margins and relegated to a separate realm called religion, where it is safely cordoned off and made to serve the interests of the reigning secular, egocentric worldview. These marginalized religious traditions, which are supposed to help us expand our spiritual horizons, are transformed into shallow, narrowly conceived entities that end up looking more like mere shadows of the secular framework that created them.

Evidence of this "shallowing" of religious traditions is all around us and too pervasive to fully describe in this short book. But of course I must highlight at least a few examples to demonstrate what I mean. Consider the growth over the last twenty years or so of evangelical megachurches being led by entertaining pastors who behave much like pop culture icons preaching the gospel of human flourishing. Americans flock to these churches by the tens of thousands to be told that God's purpose for their life is to be healthy, happy, and materially successful—exactly the message our fragile egos want to hear. Many of these megachurch leaders lack any formal academic training in theological subjects that might lend some depth to their preaching. But who needs it? Expertise in entertainment and marketing is much more important in the secular age. It is well known that the pastor of the largest church in America, the Lakewood Church in Houston, Texas, had no ministry background or theological training whatsoever before assuming leadership of this enormous congregation. Joel Osteen was running the media operation of his father's church when his father died unexpectedly and Joel stepped into the position of pastoral leadership with a pop psychology message of human flourishing that has been so successful that the church had to move into the Houston Rockets old basketball arena to accommodate the crowds (and Joel's books make the *New York Times* best-seller list)!

Of course, sending these megachurch pastors to seminary for some remedial theological study probably wouldn't do much good considering the current state of theological education in America. Depth of theological and spiritual reflection is quickly disappearing from seminary education and being replaced by an emphasis on the "practical" issues related to or-ganizing and running a church. Increasingly, pastors are seen today as or-ganizational CEOs, not as deep spiritual, theological, or prophetic figures. I hate to say it, but recent years have witnessed a real dumbing down of theological education as the demands of an increasingly shallow secular so-ciety force pastors to focus their ministries on market-driven factors. I had such a conversation with a denominational leader years ago when I was in seminary and contemplating a career in church ministry. In response to my asserting that preaching and teaching would form the primary emphasis of my work as pastor, this denominational leader responded that it would be difficult to place me in a church. When I asked why, he replied with what I thought was the stunning assertion that churches were not look-ing for strong preachers and teachers! In his understanding, congregations were seeking pastors who would emphasize evangelism and church growth. Sadly, the primary mission of too many churches revolves around strategies to get more and more people in the door and convert them to loyalty to a narrow organizational identity, with little deep reflection on what to do with them once they get there! Is it any wonder I ended up in the academy, where deep thinking is still valued (at least for now)?

Not only has religion in general, and Christianity in particular, bought into the secular emphasis on human flourishing, but this "shallowing" of religious thinking has led to a narrow exclusivism as well. I recently re-ceived a Christmas letter from a very pious pastor's wife who along with her husband and other pastoral couples had journeyed to the Middle East to learn about the causes of religious conflict in this difficult part of the world. At the end of the letter, she urged people to pray for the *Christians* in the Middle East and missionaries from her own particular denomination. Per-ish the thought that we might pray for the non-Christians (read Muslims) in the Middle East too! But of course, how often do we hear the admoni-tion "God Bless America." I suppose it would be too much to ask that God bless people in other countries as well! This narrow exclusivism stems from the growth of various forms of religious fundamentalism whereby absolute claims of truth are associated with narrowly defined religious identities, the corollary being that those who hold to a different identity are by definition wrong. Not wanting to be influenced by untruth, religious fundamentalists maintain strict boundaries between their own group and other groups, and tension and sometimes violence are the unfortunate result. One does not need to listen to an exclusivist very long to see that he or she is caught up in a narrow, superficial provisional identity designed to allay the anxiety that comes with having to engage the real ambiguity inherent in life. Fundamentalism is very much a reaction to the fear of uncertainty and ambiguity. That is, religious fundamentalists fear reality!

Another noteworthy example of this religious "shallowing" concerns the occasionally humorous arguments made by Christians in defense of the doctrine of separation of church and state. By not engaging in any deep reflection on the matter, Christian organizations like the Baptist Joint Committee on Religious Liberty demonstrate little understanding of how problematic and ambiguous the idea of separation really is. They just take for granted that religious liberty is a constitutionally guaranteed right that is worth pouring enormous resources into defending when in fact, as we saw earlier, strong arguments can be made that religious liberty is actually impossible to attain. This uncritical acceptance of church-state separation and religious liberty as goods in themselves can lead to some pretty startling conclusions.

For example, in the 1947 U.S. Supreme Court decision *Everson v. Board of Education*, the Court voted 5–4 to allow the use of taxpayer money to transport children to private Catholic schools. More specifically, the issue was whether public money could be used to support public transportation if some of the people using that transportation would be students going to religiously affiliated schools. While the Court did narrowly find this to be constitutional, strict separationists would argue otherwise. For them, maintaining the illusion (and it is an illusion) that church and state can be kept entirely separate is more important than ensuring the education of children! Is it really such an egregious error to use public funding to make sure our children can get to school and get a good education even if some of those children happen to attend academically rigorous church-affiliated schools, especially in light of the failures of public education? Where are our priorities? Proponents of separation never ask these questions. Separation of church and state is simply taken as a good in itself. There is much more to be said about the problematic nature of this illusory doctrine of church/state separation, founded as it is on the secular construction of religion as a distinct category of experience, and I will consider the issue in greater depth in chapter 5.

For now it is enough to note how the "shallowing" of religious traditions transforms them into empty identity markers, mere labels to be worn like name tags. Shorn from any connection to spiritual depth, they have very little influence on our lives and behaviors. To be sure, recent years have witnessed a wave of high-profile atheists like Sam Harris, Richard Dawkins, and Christopher Hitchens polemically blaming religion for all of the world's ills (the title of Hitchens' book *God Is Not Great: How Religion Poisons Everything* pretty much sums up this position!). But what these writers miss is the utter lack of evidence demonstrating a relationship between religious identity and behavior. These New Atheists (as they are called) are absolutely right that religious people do bad things. Muslim terrorists kill thousands of innocent people, Catholic priests sexually abuse altar boys while the Church hierarchy looks the other way, Hindu nationalists engage in terrorism. Several years ago, while touring the Medieval Torture Museum in Rothenburg, Germany, I was struck by a Latin inscription etched into the blade of a sword used to execute heretics. It read, "Soli Deo Gloria" (which also happens to be the motto of Luther College!). Execution as a God-glorifying activity! On the other hand, the New Atheists ignore the likes of Gandhi, Martin Luther King Jr., Mother Teresa, Emir Abdel Kader,[2] and innumerable other religious heroes who have selflessly given their lives over to the service of humanity.

The evidence could be multiplied many times over in defense of the thesis that religious people are capable of both heinous acts of violence and selfless acts of humanitarian love, and we find the same to be true of non-religious or secularist people too. Josef Stalin's reign of terror in the Soviet Union led to the deaths of ten million Soviet citizens. Pol Pot in Cambodia likewise slaughtered millions from an officially atheistic perspective. And we should not forget the 1989 Tiananmen Square incident in which the officially atheistic government of China slaughtered innocent protestors. Certainly, religious people are not the only ones who engage in violent behavior, nor are they the world's only humanitarians. Albert Einstein, who religiously would be considered a very secular Jew, argued vehemently

---

2. This figure is perhaps not as well known. Emir Abdel Kader was a nineteenth-century Algerian leader hailed by the pope, the Queen of England, and even Abraham Lincoln for his great humanitarian actions while resisting French colonialism. The small town of Elkader, Iowa, was even named for him. His story has been told in Kiser, *Commander of the Faithful.*

against the development of the atomic bomb (which, incidentally, was deployed by President Truman, a Christian). One of the greatest philanthropists of our day, billionaire Warren Buffett, is agnostic. And the two nineteenth-century champions of women's rights, Elizabeth Cady Stanton and Susan B. Anthony, broke with the religious traditions of their youth and adopted a humanistic stance in later life. The more we look, the clearer it becomes. There is little connection between the religious labels people wear and the kinds of behaviors they engage in. What really matters in determining behavior is not religious identity but the depth and expansiveness of a person's personality, which is not in any way tied to a particular religious identity.

Someone with a narrow, superficial view of him or herself can be Christian, Muslim, Hindu, Jewish, or any other religious identity label you can think of. And the same can be said for a person whose personality is deep and expansive. What differentiates Gandhi from Stalin or Martin Luther King from Pol Pot is not that Gandhi and King were great humanitarians because they were Hindu and Christian respectively, but because they had developed deep and expansive understandings of themselves and their callings in the world. I do not mean to imply here that the development of Gandhi's personality had nothing to do with his Hinduism nor King's with his Christianity, but simply that their behaviors stemmed from the deep and expansive personality they had developed, not from the particular religious label they wore. There can be no essential connection between King's Christian faith and his humanitarian behavior since so many other people who identify as Christian never develop the depth and expansiveness that was a hallmark of King's personality. And besides, many nonreligious people have developed deep and expansive personalities without affirming any particular religious identity.

Clearly we need a theory of human psychological development that does not arise from any particular religious worldview. Fortunately, we have a very useful one in the work of the Swiss psychoanalyst Carl Jung. In contemporary academic psychology Jung's psychodynamic approach to human development might be considered a quaint relic of a bygone era, as modern psychology focuses on the material structures of the brain and neural activity. But I will argue that the materialistic focus of contemporary psychology is itself a symptom of the larger societal movement toward secular disenchantment. In my own struggles with anxiety, nothing resonated more deeply than the Jungian paradigm, at least as it is articulated in the works of the Jungian analyst James Hollis. In what follows, I will draw heavily on his book about the proverbial midlife crisis, *The Middle Passage: From Misery to Meaning in Midlife*, which I heartily recommend to you for more detail. This little book was transformational in my journey through the darkness. Sometimes I feel as if it may have saved my life.

A Jungian Approach to Psychological Development

While I have already briefly discussed several Jungian concepts like the ego, the complex, and the Self in earlier chapters, it will be helpful here (and at the risk of repetition) to set them in the framework of Jung's larger conception of the development of the human psyche over the course of a lifetime. In places I will refer back to my own story as outlined earlier to illustrate just how closely a Jungian paradigm gives meaning to my experience. We begin once again with the idea of the provisional identity.

All of us are born into a world that is large, intimidating, and confusing. None of us asks to be born. We just arrive on the scene at a particular place and time and in the context of a particular family unit, and we have absolutely no control over any of it. As we grow, we must somehow learn to negotiate this confusing and scary terrain. Who are we and why are we here? More important perhaps, how do we figure out who we are? We begin to develop a sense of identity as children primarily through our interactions with our parents (or other primary caregivers). Do they take care of our needs? Are they nurturing and loving? Can we trust them? Do they provide us with a sense of security in a dangerous and capricious world? If we can answer these questions in the affirmative, then we probably developed a positive self-image in childhood. But try as they may, parents are never perfect, and so the self-image we develop may become tainted. Perhaps our parents worked long hours to make ends meet and did not spend enough time nurturing us. Perhaps we were faced with some type of traumatic experience they were unable to protect us from. Or perhaps they were just flat out not up to the challenge of parenting due to their own diminished psychological state (maybe they were addicted to drugs or alcohol or gambling, or just depressed like my father). No matter how hard our parents try, we all come out of childhood with a provisional identity that is mixed in terms of its functionality in the world.

Though I do have fairly happy memories of childhood, my emotionally unavailable father and overprotective mother were sending the message to me that I was incapable of negotiating the world on my own. I learned that the world was a scary place and life a mere test of endurance and that my only hope for survival was to have my mother always there to make sense of the world for me and to protect me from its capricious powers. This dynamic is crystallized for me in what I have come to call the "wet grass" incident from my childhood, a seemingly innocuous little incident that I remember so vividly it's as if it just happened yesterday. It goes like this. One morning when I was seven or eight, I asked my mother if I could go outside and play. It was a bright and sunny morning, but it had rained the night before, so assuming the grass would still be wet she granted my request with the provision that I play on the driveway and avoid getting my feet wet on the lawn. Once outside, I recognized that the sun had dried the grass. I even felt it with my hand to confirm that it was dry and then proceeded to play on it. When my mother happened to look out the window and saw me happily frolicking in the dry grass, she angrily called me in, scolding me for transgressing her orders. When I protested that the grass had dried she would hear nothing of it and only bellowed that much louder that it had rained during the night and had to still be wet. Even though I had direct knowledge about the world (I had felt the grass and knew it was dry), the message here was that my assessment of the situation could not be trusted. My assessment of the situation did not matter. Almost by definition, I was wrong and she was right. My provisional identity as someone incapable of negotiating the world on my own was set. The immense power of this formative experience continues to manifest itself in my life. Despite the fact that I am a successful college professor and have published many scholarly articles and several books, I still today find myself tending to shy away from authoritarian people, assuming that if my opinions differ from theirs I must certainly be wrong even when the evidence is on my side! I daresay we all have these innocuous childhood stories that continue to exert influence over our adult lives totally out of proportion to their seeming importance.

What makes provisional identities provisional is that we do not choose them for ourselves. They develop primarily out of how those around us respond to us, yet we internalize them as though they represent the absolute truth about who we are, and then we behave accordingly. The automatic responses that stem from these provisional identities are what Jung calls complexes. According to James Hollis,

A complex is in itself neutral, though it carries an emotional charge associated with an experiential, internalized image. The greater the intensity of the initial experience, or the longer it was reiterated, the more power the complex has in one's life. Complexes are unavoidable because one has a personal history. The problem is not that we have complexes but that complexes have us. Some complexes are useful in protecting the human organism, but others interfere with choice and may even dominate a person's life.[3]

So we all come out of childhood carrying a network of complexes, and these complexes exert tremendous influence over our lives by virtue of the fact that we are largely unaware of them. I had no clue that my dysfunctional decisions to live at home during college, to take a dead-end job at the hospital where my mother worked after college, or to move back in with my mother during graduate school after the death of my father had anything to do with a deeply internalized self-image based on my incapacity to negotiate the world on my own apart from my mother. These decisions all seemed to make sense at the time, at least to me (there *were* other people who worried about my apparent lack of desire to strike out on my own).

So we move through adolescence and into adulthood, solidifying a provisional identity as we go. Along the way our complexes may activate and lead us to make poor decisions about our lives. Perhaps we choose a career to fulfill parental expectations (we might say, "My grandfather was a doctor, my father was a doctor, so I must be a doctor even if I can't stand the sight of blood!"), or perhaps we marry the person of whom our parents most approve. Alternately, we might purposely marry the person of whom our parents most disapprove just to spite them. But either way, monumental life decisions about career and marriage are determined by parental projections, not by our own assessment of what *we* feel called to do or who *we* feel led to marry. This provisional identity, with its bevy of both functional and dysfunctional complexes, which carries us into early adulthood is what Jung calls the ego. The goal of the first part of life, in Jung's view, is to build up enough ego strength to set out on our own and begin negotiating the world independently and with some measure of confidence. Now, in earlier times when many people did not live much past the age of forty, most died while still enacting their provisional identities. But as life spans in the West have lengthened over the past century, the stage has been set for the possibility of further development beyond those provisional identities.

3. Hollis, *Middle Passage*, 13.

Much of what Jung has said to this point would probably not stir too much controversy today among psychologists. But Jung parts company with modern psychology when he addresses the second half of life. Jung is convinced that the human psyche has an infinitely expansive depth that connects in some mysterious way to the transcendence of the universe. The thing that eventually wells up from these depths and disturbs our comfortable (even if dysfunctional) ego existence is what Jung terms the Self, a mysterious constellation of energy that embodies our true identity and that at some point comes to demand expression in our lives. When the Self begins to emerge (usually around midlife), it calls into question the provisional ego identity, and this is when all hell breaks loose. Hollis writes:

> The transit of the Middle Passage occurs in the fearsome clash between the acquired personality and the demands of the Self. A person going through such an experience will often panic and say, "I don't know who I am anymore." In effect, the person one has been is to be replaced by the person to be. The first must die. No wonder there is such enormous anxiety. One is summoned, psychologically, to die unto the old self so that the new might be born.[4]

When my anxiety first broke loose, I truly felt as if I no longer knew who I was. Acknowledgment of my mother's death rendered my provisional identity utterly useless for a functional life—I now had no choice but to negotiate the world on my own, yet I truly believed I couldn't—and I was plunged into a bewildering state of utter terror and confusion. At forty-four my Middle Passage had begun in earnest, and it really did feel like a living death.

Actually, signs that the Middle Passage is beginning commonly appear long before the major symptoms erupt, but these signs are easily dismissed and ignored. Hollis describes the advent of the Middle Passage as a "kind of tectonic pressure which builds from below" like the way the plates of the earth's crust rub against each other, building up pressure until an earthquake erupts.[5] This tectonic pressure, says Hollis, "may be dismissed by defensive ego-consciousness, yet the pressure builds. Invariably, long before one becomes conscious of a crisis the signs and symptoms have been there."[6] The signs and symptoms may come in the form of mild depression,

4. Ibid., 15.
5. Ibid., 17.
6. Ibid., 17.

overindulgence in alcohol or drugs, affairs, recurrent job shifts, and other behaviors designed to ignore or outrun the growing underground pressure. I thought I was fine until my anxiety broke through late in the fall of 2004, but in retrospect the pressure had been building for the three years since my mother's death. I now realize the extent to which during those three years I had thrown myself into my work and really did not like being at home, probably because being around my wife and children served as a constant reminder of the loss of my family of origin in which my sense of identity was completely bound up. Monday mornings couldn't come fast enough so I could get back to the office and classroom, away from the reminders of my changed status. Several times when my wife was out for the evening and I was home alone with my children, a strange sense of utter loneliness washed over me and then left as quickly as it came. In June 2004, I had the opportunity to spend two weeks in Turkey to study the relationship between Islam and politics there. While I had become a pretty confident traveler, as this trip approached I became more anxious about traveling alone and suffered a full-blown panic attack in the Toronto airport, right there at the gate, while awaiting my overseas flight. I thought I was going to die right there, but magically a sense of confidence welled up just before boarding the plane and I completed the trip without further incident. The signs of the growing pressure were there long before the real crisis erupted.

While the Middle Passage usually occurs around midlife, Hollis observes that it is less a chronological event and more a psychological experience. He highlights the two different notions of time that are also employed by Charles Taylor in the latter's description of what characterizes secularism. In a secular frame we see our lives as circumscribed entirely within ordinary linear time (the *chronos*). For Hollis, "The Middle Passage occurs when the person is obliged to view his or her life as something more than a linear succession of years. The longer one remains unconscious, which is quite easy to do in our culture, the more likely one is to see life only as a succession of moments leading toward some vague end . . . .When one is stunned into consciousness, a vertical dimension, *kairos*, intersects the horizontal plane of life; one's life span is rendered in a depth perspective."[7] The Middle Passage commences when we ask, "Who am I, apart from my history and the roles I have played?"[8]

7. Ibid., 18.
8. Ibid., 19.

The confluence between Hollis's discussion of Jungian psychology and Taylor's thoughts on secularism is striking. Hollis writes that

> our culture has lost the mythic road map which helps locate a person in a larger context. Without a tribal vision of the gods, and their spiritual network, modern individuals are cut adrift to wander without guidance, without models and without assistance through the various life stages. Thus, the Middle Passage, which calls for death before rebirth, is often experienced in frightening and isolating ways, for there are no rites of passage and little help from one's peers who are equally adrift.[9]

By disenchanting the world, secularism destroys the cultural myths and rituals that might help us engage the largeness of perspective that the Self demands. Such coming of age rituals abound in indigenous cultures; one of the best descriptions appears in Malidoma Patrice Somé's fascinating and disturbing book *Of Water and Spirit: Ritual, Magic, and Initiation in the Life of an African Shaman*. This book narrates the story, set in Burkina Faso, of Somé's kidnapping by Catholic missionaries and eventual escape back to his tribal village, where he must undergo a set of elaborate initiation rituals to be accepted back into his community. In indigenous cultures, the spiritual is a reality continually experienced in everyday life. Life always has a larger framework. But alas, in our secular world, there is no larger framework to anchor us, so we wander through life just trying to get by and avoid as long as possible facing the big questions of meaning and purpose.

But for many of us, unless we have the misfortune of dying too young, the bill comes due, the Self demands expression, and crisis ensues. In fact, Hollis suggests that the psyche itself organizes the crisis and produces the resultant suffering to force upon us the recognition that our provisional identities do not represent who we truly are and must be discarded. We would never give up our provisional identities willingly and purposely bring on the suffering that ensues. Our egos will hold onto provisional identities as long as they can. When the Self demands expression, it must engineer the crisis in such a way that the only way out of the suffering is to discard our provisional identities and open fully to the larger demands of the Self, and this means opening up to the reality of a larger spiritual framework and a higher purpose. That the Self engineers the crisis of the Middle Passage is a crucial insight because one of the really troubling effects of secularism on contemporary psychology has been to transform anxiety and depression

9. Ibid., 23.

into a mental illness that must be cured with some type of behavioral or cognitive therapy or, increasingly, psychodynamic drugs. Relieving emotional suffering, however, may interfere with the process of growth. I will have more to say about this a little later in this chapter.

If we have the courage to face the suffering and resist the natural inclination to medicate it away, the suffering will lead us back to a more conscious and authentic life. No longer dominated by the projections of childhood, we become free to respond to the demands of the Self, to become who we truly are, to finally grow up and take full responsibility for our lives. Jung calls this project of the second half of life individuation. For Hollis, the entire process of the Middle Passage is beautifully encapsulated in the following story titled "Autobiography in Five Short Chapters":

I
I walk down the street.
There is a deep hole in the sidewalk.
   I fall in.
   I am lost . . . I am helpless
      It isn't my fault.
   It takes forever to find a way out.

II
I walk down the same street.
There is a deep hole in the sidewalk.
   I pretend I don't see it.
   I fall in again.
I can't believe I am in this same place.
      But it isn't my fault.
It still takes a long time to get out.

III
I walk down the same street.
There is a deep hole in the sidewalk.
   I see it is there.
   I still fall in . . . it's a habit . . . but,
      my eyes are open.
      I know where I am.
   It is *my* fault.
   I get out immediately.

IV
I walk down the same street.
   There is a deep hole in the sidewalk.

I walk around it.

V

I walk down another street.[10]

I know from experience that it can take a long time to learn to walk down another street. But when we do, we have arrived at the point of taking full responsibility for our lives and have opened ourselves entirely to the mystery of life in an incomprehensible universe.

In Jung's words, "Life is a luminous pause between two great mysteries which yet are one."[11] The purpose of the Middle Passage is to gain freedom from the dominance of the past in order to embrace the mystery of life as much as one is able. Hollis says it best:

> It is perfectly natural at midlife to feel distress about the diminution of energy and the undoing of all we have labored to secure. But underneath the distress there is an invitation. The invitation is to shift gears for the next part of the journey, to move from outer acquisition to inner development. Seen from the perspective of the first adulthood, the second half of life is a slow horror show. We lose friends, mates, children, social status, and then our lives. Yet, if it is true, as all religions attest, that the gods intend what nature knows, then we must accede to the greater wisdom of the process. Rather than operate from the perspective of youth, which can only imagine security in terms of ego, surely the greater achievement is to acquire enough tensile strength to affirm the larger rhythm of our whole lifespan.[12]

Of course, acceding to the greater wisdom of the process implies the ability to humble oneself before a greater ineffable power that we do not and cannot control. To submit to a greater power that I don't really understand is to admit that I am no longer master of my own ship and that material human flourishing cannot be the ultimate purpose of my life. Yet this is exactly the message on which our secular society is based. We are greatly in need of a collective, societal Middle Passage.

But don't hold your breath. The very people to whom we might turn for help in navigating such a passage—mental health professionals—have by and large become so secularized in their outlook that they no longer

10. Cited in Hollis, *Middle Passage*, 97. Hollis cites this as an anonymous story, but it was written by Portia Nelson and appears in her book *There's a Hole in My Sidewalk*.

11. Jung, *Letters*, 483.

12. Hollis, *Middle Passage*, 112.

believe that such a thing as a Middle Passage even exists, as I quickly learned from my first therapist, who simply could not engage the meaning of my symptoms. And this is a real loss to those who suffer through this very painful and real developmental stage of life. Anxiety and depression have been transformed from being understood as symptoms of a natural— if painful—developmental process into full-blown mental illnesses needing to be cured. And they are increasingly being treated as physical illnesses best cured by medication. This medicalization of emotional suffering, how-ever, is not based on sound science but on a questionable philosophical bias toward a secular materialist worldview. The potential harm done by the medicalization of anxiety and depression is considerable and stands as a monument to how secularization (and therefore its mirror image, religion-ization) may be helping underwrite the anxiety and depression epidemic. This important idea deserves the full elaboration that follows.

Secularism and the Mental Health System

Chances are that if you develop anxiety or depression today and seek professional help, you will not be encouraged to explore the meaning of your pain or supported through the process of connecting to the deep-est recesses of your psyche where, according to Jung, your true identity and calling lie. Jungian psychotherapy, though still practiced by some, is very much ignored by the medical and psychological establishment. Most therapists today practice some form of behavioral or cognitive therapy de-signed to reduce or eliminate symptoms and return you to a state of human flourishing. I still remember how my first therapist (a behaviorist) asked me to envision a time when I felt really good. His purpose, he said, was to help me "get back" to that place of bliss. He wanted to cure my symptoms. It shouldn't take much thought to realize how off the mark he was. The whole point is that I could not "go back." My mother's death so transformed the entire emotional terrain of my life that my only option was to move forward through the pain and emerge into a *new* place. Under the circumstances, trying to recover an earlier state would have only stunted my psychological growth. I needed to open up to a larger reality, one that transcended the narrow emotional landscape of my formative years.

But such is the state of the modern field of mental health. With the forces of secularism having cut us off from engaging the possibility that a realm of transcendence exists beyond the mundane world of our everyday experience and that our psyches might actually be connected to this transcendent realm at a deep level, anxiety and depression have been transformed into medical conditions that need to be cured, not developmental crises that might have the power to lead us to deeper, more conscious, and more expansive lives. If you tell your primary care physician that you are feeling anxious or depressed, odds are he or she will write you a prescription for an antidepressant. Mental health issues are understood today as primarily physical maladies, diseases caused by chemical imbalances in the brain that are best treated by some combination of medication and behavioral or cognitive therapy. To modern medical science, Jung is so yesterday! But the secularization and resultant medicalization of anxiety and depression may be taking a serious toll on our society. Few people, unfortunately, realize this.

As I indicated in chapter 1, I had a very ambivalent attitude toward medications during my own journey through anxiety. I desperately wanted to feel better and thought medications might help, yet I was afraid they might inadvertently drive me to commit suicide when I desperately didn't want to. So I was able to take antidepressants for only short trial periods. The first antidepressant I was prescribed was Paxil, a top-selling SSRI (selective serotonin reuptake inhibitor). After a two-week trial, it didn't seem to be having much of an effect (other than causing erectile dysfunction, a common side effect!), so my doctor switched me to Wellbutrin. While I can't say I felt less anxious on Wellbutrin, it did make me feel kind of fuzzy in the head, and it gave me a voracious appetite. I began raiding the refrigerator late in the evening, eating anything I could get my hands on. I would probably weigh three hundred pounds today if I had continued it. But not liking how it made me feel and not really trusting it, I took myself off after a couple of weeks.

I went for awhile without medication (except for the occasional Xanax), but when my condition worsened, my doctor referred me to a psychiatrist. At our first meeting, she prescribed the SSRI Lexapro with the caution that it might make me a little edgy for the first week, after which I was supposed to calm down and feel better. Well, she wasn't kidding about the initial edginess. It took only two doses before I became so agitated I had to take Xanax at night just to sleep. But that was only the beginning. The second or third day on Lexapro, I found myself sitting idly in a chair in the living room while my then four-year-old daughter was busy playing on the floor. My toddler son was napping and my wife was upstairs. As I looked over at my daughter, who was quietly amusing herself, I experienced a sudden, almost irresistible urge to physically assault her. The impulse was so strong that I didn't trust my ability to resist it, so I wisely fled out the nearest door and took a long walk to try to calm down. This helped, but as occasional disturbing urges toward physical violence continued, I called my psychiatrist and explained the situation, to which she replied, "I told you the Lexapro would make you a little edgy at first." "A little edgy!" I yelled into the phone. "I feel like I want to beat my children!" Her solution was to have me take Xanax along with the Lexapro to counteract the "edginess." Once I got past the initial edginess of the Lexapro, I could withdraw from the Xanax and begin to feel better. But the impulses toward physical violence directed at my children so terrified me that I decided I had had enough. I took myself off the Lexapro and the urges toward physical violence quickly diminished. They were clearly caused by the medication. Taking myself off of antidepressants might have been the best decision I ever made. Why?

Enter Robert Whitaker, who in 2010 authored *Anatomy of an Epidemic: Magic Bullets, Psychiatric Drugs, and the Astonishing Rise of Mental Illness in America*. Whitaker set himself the task of investigating a puzzling enigma. Everyone knows that psychiatry has made great strides in the treatment of mental illness, mostly through the psychopharmacology revolution. The release of Prozac (the first SSRI on the market) in 1988 heralded a new day in the treatment of anxiety and depression. In 2007, Americans spent $25 billion on antidepressants and antipsychotics.[13] Surely, with this revolutionary advancement in the science of mental health, one would expect the rate of mental illness to be in dramatic decline. Actually, though, the opposite is true. According to Whitaker, "as the psychopharmacology revolution has unfolded, the number of disabled mentally ill in the United States has *skyrocketed*."[14] In 1955, one in every 468 Americans was disabled by mental illness. By 1987 that number had increased to one in every 184. Since the Prozac revolution, it has risen to one in every 76 (as of 2007).[15] Even more disturbing, in 1987, mental health disability afflicted 16,200 children under the age of eighteen. By 2007, that number had ballooned to more than half a million![16] And a GAO report in 2008 concludes that

13. Whitaker, *Anatomy of an Epidemic*, 3.
14. Ibid., 5; Whitaker's emphasis.
15. Ibid., 7.
16. Ibid., 8.

one in every 16 young adults in the United States is seriously mentally ill.[17] How can the incidence of mental illness be skyrocketing in the face of all these psychiatric wonder drugs? Whitaker's disturbing conclusion is that the drugs are causing the problem!

It will require a little basic science to understand how this works. The brain is made up of billions of neurons that have tiny gaps between them called synapses. Messages are mediated from one neuron to another across the synaptic gap by chemicals called neurotransmitters. One of these neurotransmitters is serotonin, and early researchers theorized that when serotonin levels in the brain became abnormally low, it interfered with the flow of messages across the synaptic gap, which caused depression. Thus was born the notion, almost universally held today, that depression is a physical illness caused by a chemical imbalance in the brain—not enough serotonin.

When a neuron fires and releases serotonin into the synaptic gap, excess serotonin must be quickly removed to enhance the free flow of information. The neuron thus absorbs the excess serotonin back into itself in a process called reuptake. Selective serotonin reuptake inhibitors (e.g., Prozac, Paxil, Lexapro) operate, as the name implies, by blocking this reuptake process, resulting in a pileup of serotonin in the synapse. If depression is caused by low levels of serotonin, SSRIs are designed to increase these levels and thereby alleviate the depressive symptoms. But it is not so simple. When SSRIs flood the synapse with serotonin by inhibiting the natural reuptake process, the brain tries to adjust to this abnormal situation by reducing the amount of serotonin the neurons release and by reducing the number of serotonin receptors on the receiving neurons so they do not become overwhelmed by the flood of serotonin. The brain has a natural feedback mechanism designed to keep the serotonin levels in balance.

What is really disturbing here is that there is no scientific evidence that depressed people have lower levels of serotonin in their brains than nondepressed people. This is a myth that seems to have been perpetuated by a psychiatric establishment wanting to be respected as a legitimate medical specialty and a pharmaceutical industry reaping enormous profits from their bevy of psychiatric drugs. Whitaker writes in reference to research on Prozac (generic name: fluoxetine) that

> the medicine clearly doesn't *fix* a chemical imbalance in the brain. Instead, it does precisely the opposite. Prior to being medicated, a depressed person has no known chemical imbalance. Fluoxetine

17. Ibid., 10.

then gums up the normal removal of serotonin from the synapse, and that triggers a cascade of changes, and several weeks later the serotonergic pathway is operating in a decidedly *abnormal* manner.[18]

According to Whitaker, antidepressants actually *create* a chemical imbalance that was not there to begin with, and this can lead to chronic relapse and long-term disability if a person goes off the medication after being on it for a prolonged period. The drugs can cause long-lasting alterations in neural functioning.

Prior to the development of psychiatric drugs in the 1950s, depression was, according to Whitaker, a fairly rare disorder with generally good outcomes. Episodes of depression normally did not turn chronic, and most people recovered in six to twelve months (this would be consistent with a Jungian view of depression as a developmental process, though I suspect the "recovery" times were somewhat longer). But the story now is entirely different. Depression has been transformed into a widespread biological illness that needs to be treated by medication. One reason this view is convincing to so many people is that antidepressants do seem to work in the short term. Many people do feel better several weeks after beginning an antidepressant, though the outcomes literature shows that antidepressants don't significantly outperform placebos in many clinical trials. So the apparent effectiveness of antidepressants might have little to do with the medication itself, and more to do with the belief patients have that the medications will work (the placebo effect). Perhaps this is why antidepressants didn't work well for me. I manifestly did not believe in them.

But regardless of why they are effective, short-term improvement in depressive symptoms tends to level off in the longer term, and as the medications alter the neural activity of the brain, patients become more susceptible to chronic relapses, especially if they stop the medications. This can lead to chronic depression and permanent disability. Hence the solution to the enigma of why rates of depression have skyrocketed in the age of the psychopharmacology revolution. As Americans spend an estimated $25 billion on psychiatric medications, the National Institute of Mental Health reports that forty million adults suffer from anxiety, depression, or bipolar disorder. In 1955, barely more than one hundred thousand were so afflicted.

Perhaps most disturbing, Whitaker writes:

18. Whitaker, *Anatomy of an Epidemic*, 81; Whitaker's emphasis.

> As we have seen, American psychiatry has told the public a false story over the last thirty years. The field promoted the idea that its drugs fix chemical imbalances in the brain when they do no such thing, and it grossly exaggerated the merits of the second-generation psychotropics. In order to keep that tale of scientific progress afloat (and to protect its own belief in the tale), it has needed to squelch talk about the harm that the drugs can cause.[19]

Whitaker goes on to document numerous examples of the harsh discipline that has been meted out to psychiatrists who dare to question the prevailing chemical imbalance theory (despite the fact that there is no scientific basis for it). He also gives disturbing examples of the lavish perks bestowed by the pharmaceutical industry on those psychiatrists who provide "expert" testimony in favor of the theory.

That the mental health establishment has not been straight with the public about the benefits and risks of antidepressant medications is documented in a disturbing study published in the venerable *New England Journal of Medicine* in 2008. In a study of seventy-four FDA-registered clinical trials for thirteen different antidepressants, the authors found that only 69 percent of those trials were ever published—the 69 percent that indicated a positive outcome! These were the clinical trials in which antidepressants outperformed placebos in a statistically significant way. The 31 percent of trials that were never published were in most cases trials lacking a positive outcome. So according to the *published* literature, it appeared that 94 percent of clinical trials produced positive results when in fact only 51 percent actually did. The authors concluded, "Not only were positive results more likely to be published, but studies that were not positive, in our opinion, were often published in a way that conveyed a positive outcome."[20] The lack of clear and unambiguous clinical evidence for the superiority of antidepressants over placebos is such an embarrassment to the pharmaceutical industry that it needs to distort the results of clinical trials to hide this fact! In the understated manner of the medical journal genre, the authors finally conclude that "selective reporting of clinical trial results may have adverse consequences for researchers, study participants, health care professionals, and patients."[21] No kidding!

19. Ibid., 304.
20. Turner et al., "Selective Publication," 256.
21. Ibid., 252.

Now, I am not suggesting in all this that antidepressants are never warranted. Heaven knows my father would likely not have recovered from his crippling depression without them (but this was in the pre-SSRI days). Certainly there are times when medication is probably necessary, but doctors today are writing prescriptions for virtually every patient who walks into their office complaining of feeling a little down or a bit anxious. The secular framework of our lives has driven us to become so enamored with human flourishing as the ultimate goal of life that we feel entitled to the avoidance of psychic pain at all costs. How can we flourish when we are anxious or depressed? Feeling a little anxious or feeling a little sad? No need to suffer. There's a pill for that. Unfortunately, the pills may make us worse over the long run, which is why I am so thankful that my anxiety made it impossible for me to take medication for my anxiety! I recovered without pills just as people did in the pre-medication days. Of course, this recovery took time and was far from easy, but where in the world did we ever get the idea that life is supposed to be easy? The pursuit of a life of ease is a corollary to the pursuit of human flourishing. James Hollis believes it is necessary to occasionally wade into what he calls the "swamplands of the soul." To avoid pain is to forfeit the possibility of developing the kind of spiritual depth that might make us less susceptible to further bouts of anxiety and depression in the long run.

Robert Whitaker is not a lone voice in the critique of the psychopharmacology revolution. A number of books have been published over the last five years trying to pull back the veil on the tragic societal myth that anxiety and depression are primarily medical conditions. I like how Gary Greenberg, a psychotherapist and himself a depression sufferer, says it in his book *Manufacturing Depression: The Secret History of a Modern Disease*:

> Call your sorrow a disease or don't. Take drugs or don't. See a therapist or don't. But whatever you do, when life drives you to your knees, which it is bound to do, which maybe it is meant to do, don't settle for being sick in the brain. Remember that's just a story. You can tell your own story about your discontents, and my guess is that it will be better than the one that the depression doctors have manufactured.[22]

I want to advocate for a recovery of the old Jungian story. The medicalization of anxiety and depression arises from the secular demand that all things be understood within the framework of the material realm. In this

22. Greenberg, *Manufacturing Depression*, 367.

story the profoundly complex landscape of human emotional life must be the result of nothing more than the biochemical processes of a material brain. And the hubris it takes to believe that we can control this complex emotional landscape by material means—by medication—and magically banish all suffering from life just demonstrates how triumphant our collective egos have become.

But as we saw in our summary of the Jungian paradigm, living entirely from the ego robs us of our appointment with the Self, that mysterious complex of energy at the core of our psyches that holds within it our true identities and the possibility of connection to transcendence. Connecting to the Self and the possibility of transcendence, of course, requires moving beyond the ego—with its bevy of provisional identities, including our religious identities—and enduring for a time the tremendous anxiety that results from this identity crisis. It would be nice if our society were set up to support this journey of the soul, but alas, we are largely left to go it alone in a secular realm that has given up on the possibility of transcendence. It is not easy to go it alone, but:

> When we grasp the wheel on the captain's deck, scarce knowing our direction, knowing only that the thing must be done, then we live the high adventure of the soul. In the long run, it is the only journey worth taking. The task of the first half of life is to attain sufficient ego strength to leave parents and enter the world. This strength becomes available in the second half for the larger journey of the soul. Then the axis shifts from ego-world to ego-Self and the mystery of life unfolds in ever renewing ways. This is not a denial of our social reality but a restoration of the essentially religious character of our lives.[23]

James Hollis, who wrote the above passage, is fond of pointing out how Jung's basic question boils down to asking of a person, "Is he related to something infinite or not? That is the telling question of his life."[24] If there is a cure for anxiety, it is to become radically open to the infinite expanse of our own psyches. But this will require transcending the boundaries of the narrowly defined religious identities that help lock us into the prison of ego-induced secularism. How do we make this transition, and what barriers must we overcome?

---

23. Hollis, *Middle Passage*, 99.
24. Jung, *Memories, Dreams, Reflections*, 325.

Barriers to a Radically Open Life

Since religious identity only has meaning in a secular world; and since secularism, by its very nature, fosters the development of a narrow and shallow worldview; and since a narrow and shallow worldview creates the conditions for an anxiety epidemic, we should have every reason to want to move beyond our narrowly conceived religious identities. But this is not easy to do in a society structured in a way diametrically opposed to such a movement. Our lives are so filled with the clutter and distractions of consumerism and technology that we barely ever have any time to truly be alone, where the meeting with the Self can occur. We have become trapped in a prison of superficiality characterized by a reliance on the cryptic and the inane. We text, apparently so we don't have to go to the trouble of spelling out entire words! We tweet, a form of communication that requires us to keep our messages as short and cryptic as possible. And when we really crave human connection, we turn to Facebook, where we can "friend" people we have never met and be bedazzled by their inane and mundane posts. Do our "friends" really need to be informed of every little thought that crosses our minds? (I should disclose that I actually do have a Facebook account—this is how I know what people post there—but I refuse to text or tweet!) We are quickly losing the ability to converse in a deep and meaningful way on any important issue. I am continually struck by how often I see students walking together across our college campus, each one on a cell phone talking to someone who isn't there and ignoring each other. Recently I took my son to an elementary school basketball clinic and was shocked to notice how many parents had their eyes glued to their cell phones; they were texting to pass the time rather than watching what their children were doing on the court.

More seriously, this shallowing of our worldview is negatively influencing our political discourse, rendering it nearly impossible to address the serious issues that threaten the very future of this country and the sustainability of the entire planet. Political arguments have been reduced to sound bites and political debates to name-calling. Adherence to narrowly defined political identities has advanced to such a degree that it is no longer necessary for any political figure to develop a substantive argument in defense of a policy position. Politicians merely state their position; rarely, if ever, are they called on to argue or defend it. Conservatives bash liberal positions simply because they are held by liberals, and liberals decry conservative ideas because they are conservative ideas. The ability to look past the labels and grapple with the real complexity of issues like economic insecurity, tense international relations, and global climate change is fast disappearing. We have to remember that there are no conservative or liberal positions on anything. There are just varying viewpoints on issues. "Conservative" and "liberal" are merely interpretive labels that we place on these viewpoints in part so we don't have to bother dealing with the complexity and ambiguity that would threaten the foundation of our simplistic, ego-ordered world.

Of course, at some level we crave all this distracting clutter and the superficiality it creates because, truth be told, we are afraid of the meeting with the Self. While at one level we may recognize the problems with our secular age, at a deeper level we fear the unknown and the profound depths of our own souls. We don't know what we will find there or what our souls will require of us. Jung recognized that the tendency to devalue the psyche and to resist psychological enlightenment is "based in large measure on fear—on panic fear of the discoveries that might be made in the realm of the unconscious."[25] Without a societal structure in place to encourage the development of a depth dimension to our lives, like what we often find in indigenous societies, our only choice is to face the fear by ourselves, disconnect from the distractions, and give ourselves the gift of aloneness so that the deepening of the spirit can occur. It is not ideal, but it is the best we can do at present.

But perhaps the hardest part is to allow ourselves to venture beyond the borders of our religious identities. Many narrowly religious people have become so conditioned to believe that truth can only be encountered within the bounds of their own tradition—and in the minds of some, eternal damnation awaits anyone outside that tradition—that it feels like absolute apostasy even to consider venturing beyond the borders. Of course, if fear is the primary motivation that forces us to remain within narrowly conceived religious identity borders, we might well question whether maintaining these borders is really in our best interest. And it would be helpful if we paid more attention to the permeability of these religious borders. Actually, it is amazing how little we recognize the emptiness of religious labels and the permeability of religious boundaries.

Christianity in all its manifold forms, of course, revolves around the life and work of a first-century Jew named Jesus. Jesus never identified himself, nor was he ever identified by others, as a Christian. The same is true of the Apostle Paul, who lived and died fully within the Jewish tradition.

25. Jung, *Undiscovered Self*, 49.

Martin Luther, the force behind the Protestant Reformation, was not a Lutheran. He was a Catholic until the day he died. The founder of Methodism, John Wesley, was always an Anglican. The same is certainly true for important figures in other religious traditions as well. While the fourth Islamic Caliph, Ali, is a central figure within the Shi'ite form of Islam, there is no sense in which Ali was himself a Shi'ite since there is no evidence of the formation of a distinctly Shi'ite form of Islam until well after Ali's life. So if Christians worship a Jew, Lutherans follow a Catholic, Methodists follow an Anglican, and Shi'ites follow a Sunni, does it really make much sense to pour so much energy into policing these rigid borders between traditions?

The profound irony of all this is unmistakable. If narrowly defined religious identities are the product of the secularized world, as I have argued is the case, then adherence to them entails acquiescence to the very demands of secularism. Yet it is superficially religious people who tend to be the most vocal critics of secularism! Do these people realize they are acquiescing to the very system they decry? Do they realize that by confining spiritual truth to a narrowly conceived set of doctrines, creeds, or scriptures, they are bowing before the lords of secular society who demand that any reference to transcendence be removed from the scientific, political, economic, and social spheres of life, where it might actually help us address issues of war, poverty, environmental destruction, and many other issues of global injustice? Sadly, they don't realize this because the secular mindset that constructs religion as a separate sphere of life is so deeply ingrained in our thinking that to challenge it almost seems like heresy. And who wants to be branded a heretic (other than all those transformative religious figures of the past!)? At the risk of numbering myself among the heretics, I will challenge this fundamental notion, for there is ample evidence to show that many people throughout history and in the contemporary world did not and do not view the world through the lens of this religious/secular dichotomy. There are other options. As surprising as it may seem in these days of Islamophobic mania, I will hold up the Islamic tradition as one that suggests resources for how to escape the trap of secularism and restore a desperately needed depth dimension to life, thereby opening us up to a larger perspective that might reduce our anxiety and lead to the creation of a more humane world. How might the Islamic tradition suggest resources for helping us transcend the narrow confines of religious identity and become radically open? I will now consider this question in detail.

four

Islam and the Transcendence of Religious Identity

SHORTLY AFTER THE 2009 publication of my book *Was Jesus a Muslim?*, I was having lunch with a friend at a small cozy bistro with a copy of my book lying face up on the table. As a waitress approached the table to take our order, her eyes fell on the cover and the question posed in the title. She paused, shook her head, uttered a barely audible—but nevertheless emphatic—"No!" and walked away, momentarily forgetting that there were customers at the table! This brief episode beautifully illustrates the difficulty inherent in constructions of religious identity. The mere suggestion that Jesus could be considered anything other than a Christian (even though he manifestly wasn't) was too much for this waitress to bear. We normally view people as being adherents of only one religion at any given time since the boundaries between religions are treated as being hard, fast, and mutually exclusive. If you are a Christian you can't possibly be a Muslim. If you are Jewish, you can't possibly be Buddhist. The reaction of this waitress to the question, "Was Jesus a Muslim?" is hardly unique among Christians. There is little evidence that my book has sold particularly well within the Christian community. Questioning Jesus's standard religious categorization—especially raising the specter that he may have been a Muslim—is just too provocative.

Interestingly, reaction to my book within the Muslim community has been altogether different. Shortly after the book appeared, I received an e-mail from a Muslim religion scholar informing me that he had only gotten to page twenty and just had to stop to let me know how wonderful he thought the book was. This was followed a few days later by a phone call from the Emir of the Islamic Organization of North America (IONA) thanking me for writing the book and saying that I wrote about Islam in a way that he had encountered in few other non-Muslim writers. He was effusive in his praise, and before I knew it he was inviting me to IONA's suburban Detroit headquarters to present my ideas to the Muslim community there. That event went so well that IONA began setting up speaking engagements for me in mosques all across North America—in Raleigh, Santa Clara, Sacramento, Toronto, Las Vegas, and other places. While Christians approach my work with great trepidation, Muslims have embraced it with considerable enthusiasm. It turns out the question at the heart of the book is not at all controversial among Muslims, who readily accept Jesus' Muslim identity as an article of faith (Jesus appears more than ninety times in the Qur'an). What surprises Muslims is to hear this question being answered in the affirmative by someone who identifies as a Christian (though I don't employ the term *Christian* as a religious identity label). Most Muslims have never met a Christian quite like me.

The starkly different reactions by Christians and Muslims to my work are profoundly illustrative. Muslims and Christians both agree that Jesus lived six hundred years before the advent of Islam in seventh-century Arabia. Both agree that it is chronologically impossible that Jesus recited the Qur'an, fasted during Ramadan, or made a pilgrimage to Mecca. Jesus never set foot in a mosque, he never said the five daily prayers facing Mecca, nor did he confess the Shahadah (the Muslim profession of faith). For Christians, these clear and agreed-upon facts negate the possibility that Jesus could have been a Muslim, but for Muslims they don't. Why not? Are Muslims just simply blind to the evidence or stubbornly unwilling to accept it? Not at all. The answer is really quite simple and does not require casting aspersions on Muslims (as much as people like to do that these days). The assertion "Jesus was a Muslim" is not generally taken by Muslims to be an assertion of religious identity, whereas for Christians it is. A Muslim who states "Jesus was a Muslim" is not indicating a belief that Jesus followed the five pillars of Islam or recited the Qur'an in Arabic. The concept "Muslim" has not been understood historically within the Islamic tradition to function as a specifically religious identity label. Of course, this startling idea raises the larger question: What *does* a Muslim mean to indicate by identifying Jesus as a Muslim? I will address this central question here, for the answer will reveal a critical insight into what it would mean to transcend religious identity and live the kind of radically open life that might create the more expansive personality envisioned by Jung as the "cure" for anxiety.

Islam and the Problem of Religion

There is an oft-repeated dictum among Muslims that goes, "Islam is not a religion, it is a way of life." This dictum has been repeated so often that it has become a mere cliché, which is unfortunate since it actually points to a truly profound insight. As we saw earlier, *religion* is a very troublesome word. It lacks any clear definition and appears not to pick out any real entity existing in the world that could be distinguished from non-religion. The categorization of some traditions as religions—be they Christianity, Islam, capitalist economics, professional football, or the Church of the Flying Spaghetti Monster—is an entirely arbitrary process and one often resulting from profoundly political struggles. There really are no useful distinctions to be made between religious, political, or economic processes. We merely talk as if these are clearly distinguishable entities. Given the problematic nature of the generic concept "religion," we should sit up and take notice of this oft-repeated Muslim denial. Maybe Muslims know something that we in the West have yet to learn.

My first encounter with the Muslim denial of Islam as a religion came through an interaction with a Muslim student during my first year of teaching at Luther College. I was teaching an introductory course on Islam using the comparative religion approach I had learned in my graduate school studies, but there happened to be a young Muslim woman from Morocco who came by my office late in the semester to register her discomfort with how I was teaching her religious tradition. At first she was unable to articulate exactly what was wrong with my approach to Islam. She just had a gut feeling that something was amiss. As I worked closely with her over the next couple of years (all of this happening in the first two years after the 9/11 attacks), it became apparent that what she was reacting to was my characterization of Islam as one of the world's great religions. In her mind, Islam was not a religion; it was—here we go again—a way of life. At first I protested, saying, "What do you mean Islam is not a religion? Courses on Islam are taught in the religion departments of colleges and universities all over North America. Every textbook on world religions has a chapter devoted to Islam. What do you mean Islam is not a religion?" She replied more firmly, "Islam is not a religion." Her questioning forced me to reassess much of what I thought I knew about religion, and I came, over time, to understand what she was getting at. The Muslim denial of religion is a truly profound idea, as I hope to show in what follows.

At the outset, let me be clear that I am not saying that all Muslims everywhere deny that Islam constitutes a specific, exclusive religious identity. This is obviously not the case. As secularism has overtaken large parts of the world in recent generations, Islam has been effectively transformed into a religious identity in the minds of many millions of Muslims. Where Christians and Jews meet various kinds of oppression in Muslim-majority countries, it is likely that many Muslims in these places do in fact view Islam as in some sense a rival religion to Christianity and Judaism (compare this with the noted *convivencia* of medieval Spain where Christians and Jews lived quite well under the auspices of an Islamic empire). In certain forms of "fundamentalist" Islam like that of the Taliban in Afghanistan or Wahabbism in Saudi Arabia, Islam has devolved in the minds of many adherents to the level of being a rather superficial exclusive claim to religious identity. The level to which this has happened demonstrates just how strong and pervasive the influence of secularism has become throughout the world. Recall that it is secularism that creates religion, so Islam can only be understood as a religious identity in the context of a secular society. But secularism is a rather modern phenomenon, and what is true of many Muslims today was not necessarily true of Muslims of the past, and there is very good evidence to suggest that Islam did not arise in seventh-century Arabia as a new specifically religious movement. But if it was not a religion, what was it?

The Character of Early Islam

The easiest way to assess the character of the early Islamic movement is to consider the worldview described in the Muslim scriptures, the Qur'an. The Qur'an is understood by Muslims to be a collection of divine revelations mediated to the prophet Muhammad by the angel Gabriel over a period of some twenty-two years, from 610–632 CE. In recent times, some Western scholars have painted a more skeptical picture of the Qur'an, placing its origin generations beyond the earliest Muslim community, meaning that the worldview emanating from it represents that of the later Muslim community, not that of the nascent movement. But more recently, the usefulness of the Qur'an for reconstructing Muslim origins has found support in the work of Fred M. Donner, a highly respected historian of the Islamic tradition who teaches at the University of Chicago. I will consider his book *Muhammad and the Believers: At the Origins of Islam* in some detail below.

First, let's look directly at a few qur'anic texts to get a sense of how the Qur'an views the character of the early Islamic movement.

I begin with Surah 45:24 (the Qur'an is divided into 114 surahs or chapters):

> And yet they say: "There is nothing beyond our life in this world.
>   We die as we come to life, and nothing but time destroys us."
> But of this they have no knowledge whatever;
>   they do nothing but guess.[1]

In this one short verse the Qur'an alludes to the insights about secularism that we drew out in chapter 2 from the work of Charles Taylor. The opponents of Islam, this verse seems to suggest, live entirely within a chronological understanding of time. Life is just a succession of days leading to death, and all human life is circumscribed by an earthly frame of reference. The Qur'an, however, views Islam as the antithesis of this secular viewpoint. The Qur'an reveals the existence of an overarching power—Allah—to which we humans owe our very existence and to which we are called to willingly submit our lives in totality. Our lives, according to the Qur'an, should be circumscribed by a much larger, more expansive frame of reference (a very Jungian idea!).

This is a crucial insight. If Islam, understood as the act of submitting to a greater power, is being put in opposition to a secular worldview that cannot see beyond a material earthly realm, then Islam is understood within the Qur'an as in some sense a replacement for secularism. But if, as I have argued, religion and secularism are created together and each is mutually dependent upon the other for its existence, then if Islam replaces secularism it will replace religion too, and hence Islam cannot itself be understood as just another type of religion along with Christianity, Judaism, Buddhism, Hinduism, etc. Islam is simultaneously the antithesis of secularism and the antithesis of religion! The Qur'an manifestly does not portray Islam as one religion among a number of other religions. Islam is a different order of thing. But what?

The Qur'an consistently characterizes Islam using the Arabic word *din*. In a number of verses Islam is said to be Allah's *din*. But this is where much of the confusion begins. The word *din*, which really has no good English equivalent, has generally been translated into English as "religion." Patrice Brodeur, writing in *The Encyclopedia of the Qur'an*, states:

1. Qur'anic interpretations are from Asad, *The Message of the Qur'an*, unless otherwise noted.

> Prior to the twentieth century, the English word "religion" had no direct equivalent in Arabic nor had the Arabic word *din* in English. They became partially synonymous only in the course of the twentieth century as a result of increased English-Arabic encounters and the need for consistency in translation.[2]

According to Brodeur, current global power dynamics are having the effect of making sure that the meaning associated with the English word *religion* is being increasingly imposed on the Arabic *din* rather than vice versa. Given the complexity of the two words in their respective linguistic and historical contexts, he warns that "the primary danger to avoid is the simplistic reduction of the Arabic word *din* to that of the English 'religion.'"[3]

If there *is* a word in the Qur'an that is in any way equivalent to the English word *religion* (and it is not clear that there is), it is *milla*, not *din*. The term *milla* seems to convey some sense of a particular confessional community, and as such it is used to refer to both Christians and Jews in Surah 2:120 ("For never will the Jews be pleased with thee, nor yet the Christians, unless you follow their own *milla*"). Islam is never referred to as a *milla*, so clearly the Qur'an views Islam as being a different order of thing. Islam is a *din*, Judaism and Christianity are *millas*. A number of verses do employ *milla* to describe Abraham's correct response to the divine call to submit, and in three places (Surahs 4:125, 6:161, and 22:78), *milla* and *din* appear in the same verse. For example, 6:161:

> Say: "Behold, my Sustainer has guided me onto a straight way
> through an ever-
> true *din*—the *milla* of Abraham, who turned away from all
> that is false . . ."

Here *din* denotes a straight way, a comprehensive, divinely ordained structure for all aspects of life. The *milla* of Abraham represents the correct human response to living within Allah's *din*. And what is the correct human response to the reality of Allah? It is submission (*islam*). Muslims, then, are simply those who engage in that act of submission.

What causes so much confusion is the distinction between uppercase and lowercase letters so fundamental to the English language. Words like *Islam* and *Muslim* are spelled with uppercase letters in order to denote a specific confessional identity. But Arabic does not make the uppercase/lowercase distinction, so the Arabic words *islam* and *muslim* in the Qur'an may

2. Brodeur, "Religion," 395.
3. Ibid.

very well not be markers of confessional identity but merely generic terms denoting a particular act, attitude, or orientation to life—that of submission. Consider the following usages of *muslim* in the Qur'an.

In Surah 10:90, we meet the story, familiar from the Bible, of Pharaoh pursuing the liberated Hebrew slaves through the Red Sea. At the point of being overwhelmed by the flood waters, Pharaoh cries out, "I have come to believe that there is no deity save Him in whom the children of Israel believe, and I am of those who surrender themselves [*muslim*] unto Him!" This use of *muslim* cannot denote the confessional identity "Muslim" since Pharaoh lived long before any identifiable Muslim movement existed. The Qur'an understands Pharaoh to be merely pointing out an attitude or action he is engaging in—that of submission to the God of Israel. In a similar way, Surah 12:101 portrays Joseph, the son of Jacob known so well from the biblical saga in the book of Genesis, as beseeching God to "let me die as one who has surrendered himself [*muslim*] unto Thee, and make me one with the righteous!" Surah 51:36 has Lot reporting to Abraham during the Sodom and Gomorrah episode that he has been able to find submitters (*muslim*) in only one house. Obviously, Lot would be hard-pressed to find confessionally specific Muslims more than two thousand years prior to the advent of the Muslim community in seventh-century Arabia! By repeatedly referring to pre-Islamic figures using the Arabic word *muslim*, the Qur'an must be using this word in a generic, not a specifically confessional, sense.

In Surah 29:46, the grammatical context *requires* that *muslim* be understood as a generic reference to the act of submission (or surrender, as Asad has it), not a unique confessional identity. The receivers of the revelation are instructed to say to the People of the Book,

> We believe in that which has been bestowed from on high upon us,
>> as well as that which has been bestowed upon you:
> for our God and your God is one and the same,
>> and it is unto Him that we surrender ourselves [*muslim*].

It would make little sense grammatically to say "to him we are Muslims," referring to a distinct confessional identity. Clearly *muslim* has a verbal force here—"to him we surrender ourselves." Finally, in Surah 72:14, we read, "Yet [it is true] that among us are such as have surrendered themselves [*muslim*] to God—just as there are among us such as have abandoned themselves to wrongdoing." By placing *muslim* in opposition to "abandon themselves to wrongdoing," the Qur'an clearly understands *muslim* to refer to a generic action (the opposite of abandoning themselves to wrongdoing) that could apply to anyone, not a specific confessional identity applying only to those who practice the five pillars.

Given this evidence and the fact that Arabic makes no distinction between uppercase *m* Muslim and lowercase *m* muslim, it is almost certain that the forty-two occurrences of *muslim* in the Qur'an should all be interpreted generically as denoting the attitude and action of surrendering entirely to God. Said another way, there is no evidence that the receivers of the qur'anic revelation—those we would refer to as Muslims today—were ever addressed originally with any kind of particular religious title in the Qur'an itself! The Qur'an simply does not portray Islam as a new, mutually exclusive religious entity in conflict with the already existing religious entities encountered in seventh-century Arabia. In fact, strong evidence supports the notion that islam (with a small *i*) arose as an ecumenical movement that included Jews, Christians, Zoroastrians, and any others willing to live a life of submission to one God. This is the view, at least, of Fred M. Donner, author of *Muhammad and the Believers*, referred to above.

According to the traditional narrative of Muslim origins, Islam originated in Mecca in 610 CE when then forty-year-old Muhammad received his first revelation commissioning him to call his fellow Meccans to forsake the polytheistic tribal deities they worshipped in the form of idols and submit only to the supreme creator God (*Allah* means "The God"). This message of submission had profound social, political, and economic implications for the Meccans since it was essentially calling them to utterly transform their entire way of life. Allegiance to tribe and clan and the honor/shame ethic that caused so much bloodshed was to be replaced by allegiance to one God. The existence of one God implied the unity of all humanity living in submission to this single deity. Furthermore, forsaking idol worship was experienced as a direct economic threat to those who made their living manufacturing the idols and overseeing polytheistic worship at the central shrine in Mecca, known as the Ka'ba. Not surprisingly, then, Muhammad's preaching was met with great resistance, a resistance that might have proved fatal had he not emigrated in 622 CE about two hundred miles north to the desert oasis town of Yathrib (which would come to be known as Medina).

His preaching found fertile soil in this oasis enclave, and Muhammad's movement grew quickly in numbers. This alarmed his Meccan adversaries, and a series of battles eventually led to Muhammad's muslim movement subduing the Meccans. In short order, Muhammad found himself leading a movement that was transforming life throughout the Arabian Peninsula and that would continue to transform a good chunk of the world after his untimely death in 632 CE. But what exactly was the character of this movement?

While he accepts the general outline of this traditional narrative of Islamic origins, historian Donner offers some startling revisions to some of the details. First, he observes that the Qur'an addresses its message to people it refers to as *mu'minun* (believers) almost a thousand times compared to the relative paucity of references to *muslimun* (a mere forty-two times). Anyone reading the Qur'an will quickly come to recognize the repeated phrase "O you who believe." It stands to reason then that the earliest followers of Muhammad's message about submission did not call themselves muslims at all, but rather believers. And this "Believers' movement," as Donner calls it, was likely a diverse monotheistic reform movement that included any who engaged in submission to one God regardless of what other ethnic or religious identity they may have ascribed to. Donner writes:

> As used in the Qur'an, then, *islam* and *muslim* do not yet have the sense of confessional distinctness we now associate with "Islam" and "Muslim"; they meant something broader and more inclusive and were sometimes even applied to some Christians and Jews, who were, after all, monotheists.[4]

The suggestion that early muslims understood themselves not as Muslims (but as believers) may seem a bit strange, and perhaps a little hard to swallow if you are a contemporary Muslim. But Donner offers interesting documentary evidence to support this intriguing idea.

Western scholars have traditionally portrayed the expansion of Islam as being carried out at the tip of a sword. According to this view, non-Muslims were forced to convert to Islam or face violent conquest through the waging of Holy War. But Donner challenges this depiction, partly because little evidence exists of these military conquests. Archaeological excavations have turned up little or no evidence of destruction or other forms of violence in these lands. It rather appears that

> the area underwent a gradual process of social and cultural transformation that did not involve a violent and sudden destruction of urban or rural life at all. In town after town, we find evidence of churches that are not destroyed—but, rather, continue in use

---

4. Donner, *Muhammad and the Believers*, 71.

for a century or more after the "conquest"—or evidence that new churches (with dated mosaic floors) were being constructed.[5]

According to Donner, if Islam constituted a religious confessional movement demanding conversion of conquered peoples, the adherents of Christianity and other religions would almost certainly have resisted, and that resistance surely would have left its marks in the literature of the period. "But no significant Christian or other polemics against the Believers' doctrines appear for almost a century."[6]

The evidence is compelling and difficult to square with the idea that Islam was a confessional religious movement in direct competition with other confessional movements like Christianity and Judaism. But if the Believers were what Donner refers to as an "ecumenical" monotheistic reform movement, the evidence begins to make sense. Donner writes:

> The predominantly West-Arabian leaders of the Believers' movement were not asking the people of Syria-Palestine, Egypt, and Iraq to give up their ancestral religion to embrace another—that surely would have led to violent confrontation. But they were imposing their political hegemony on the conquered populations, requiring them to pay taxes, and asking them, at least initially, to affirm their belief in one God and in the Last Day, and to affirm their commitment to living righteously and to avoid sin. They were, in short, establishing a new political order and perhaps advancing a program of monotheistic (and moral?) reform but not proposing religious revolution or demanding conversion to a new faith.[7]

Perhaps the most compelling bit of evidence supporting Donner's depiction of Islam as an ecumenical movement revolves around documentary evidence concerning the Shahadah.

The Shahadah is the basic confession of faith in Islam, and recitation of it the first pillar of the faith. It goes, "There is no God but The God, and Muhammad is the messenger of The God." If anything captures the essence of Islam it is the Shahadah. This confession expresses the unity of God and the unique status of Muhammad as the final Messenger of God. Yet Donner claims that the earliest documentary evidence of the Shahadah found on coins, papyri, and inscriptions dated before about 685 CE (remember Muhammad died in 632) includes only the first half of the Shahadah ("There is

5. Ibid., 107.
6. Ibid., 109.
7. Ibid., 109–10.

no God but The God"). Muhammad is not mentioned![8] If the full form of the Shahadah as we know it today formed the basis for the Believers' movement from the beginning, surely there would be documentary evidence for it. It is hard to escape the conclusion that the nascent islamic movement did not coalesce around a distinct confessional identity. It was a movement to call people to a new orientation toward life, a life of complete and utter submission to a unified deity with all the spiritual, social, political, and economic implications such submission entailed.

Donner goes on to argue that over time, the Believers' movement began to lose its ecumenical character, and by the Umayyad period (661–750 CE) a more distinctly Muslim identity emerged. The Umayyad caliph Abd al-Malik began minting coins bearing the full form of the Shahadah, and the beautiful Dome of the Rock he built in Jerusalem contains many inscriptions mentioning Muhammad.[9] As Islam morphs first into a monarchy and then into an empire, it develops a more distinct confessional identity. But this was not a characteristic of the original movement. But the nature of Abd al-Malik's confessionalization of Islam is somewhat ambiguous. For the Dome of the Rock contains inscriptions asserting not only the messengership of Muhammad, but also that of Jesus ("For the Messiah Jesus, son of Mary, is the messenger of God"). And even as late as the middle of the eighth century it is not clear that non-Muslims recognize Islam to be a religion distinct from Christianity. The Christian writer John of Damascus, who served as a high administrator in the Umayyad dynasty, wrote a treatise on "The Heresy of the Ishmaelites."[10] Heresy is a specifically Christian term used to denote deviant forms of Christianity, not entire new religions. Finally, we cannot ignore Surah 2:62:

> Verily, those who have attained to faith [in this divine writ], as well as those who
> follow the Jewish faith, and the Christians, and the Sabians—all who believe in God and the Last Day and do righteous deeds—shall have their reward with their Sustainer . . .

The early Islamic movement was open and ecumenical. It was open to any "who have attained faith."

8. Donner, *Muhammad and the Believers*, 112.

9. Ibid., 205.

10. Ibid., 223.

The Islamization of Daily Life

Given the evidence above, perhaps we should no longer refer to the development of a religion called Islam but rather to the development of a movement of islamization. Muhammad did not attempt to found a new religious community but rather a dynamic movement designed to fundamentally alter people's orientation to life away from reliance on tribal identities tied to deities worshipped in the form of idols toward a radically open posture of submission to an all-pervading power of the universe. Effecting such a reorientation is difficult, however, since it requires people to willingly give up restrictive provisional identities and submit to a higher power that they neither fully understand nor control and that may require of them more than they are willing to give. We have already seen how hesitant people are to do this. It is therefore not surprising that this dynamic movement of reorientation fairly quickly devolved into a more static entity bearing a specific confessional identity—Islam—that could be distinguished from other confessional identities—Christianity, Judaism, etc. This static entity came to rely more and more on human power and control in the form of monarchy, thus forsaking the idea of radical human openness and submission to nonhuman power—God. But despite the difficulty of remaining true to the original spirit of Islam (or more correctly *islam*), Muslim scholars have never given up hope of bringing about a global reorientation to a life of submission.

This is a point of great misunderstanding that helps fuel so much of the antipathy toward Islam in the West. People hear that Muslims want to "Islamize" the world and automatically interpret this as a call to convert the global population to the religion of Islam. Muslims are accused of wanting to destroy Christianity, impose shari'a (Islamic law) on every country, and create a single worldwide religion. They are accused of wanting to transform political and economic systems in accordance with Islamic sympathies, a charge that supports the stereotype of Muslims as being too political in their faith. Muslims, we are told, need to recognize that Islam is a religion and keep it separate from politics and economics like we do here in the West (except that we don't!). That is, Muslims need to respect the separation of mosque and state. Clearly, there are individual Muslims who would convert everyone to a narrow confessional Muslim identity if they could. But this is not the way the process of islamization is viewed by a host of important Islamic thinkers.

For them, islamization is about bringing about a reorientation toward life. It is about constructing a world where people live in submission to divine rather than human power and authority, something that people can do no matter what religious identity label they happen to wear. But for this type of reorientation to occur, it can't just be something that individual people decide to do on their own power. It takes more than simple intellectual or emotional assent to live in submission to a higher power and authority. Why? Because all of the structures that we surround ourselves with—the political, economic, educational and others—are specifically designed to undermine a life of submission and to keep us beholden to a secular life centered on human authority and human material flourishing. For islamization to be effective, then, it must involve not only the transformation of individual human attitudes, but also the transformation of societal structures to reinforce and bring about those changes in individual attitude.

Insight on why this is so comes from an unlikely source, the writings of Karl Marx. Whatever you think of Marx (many of the ideas ascribed to him he never actually held!), he understood as well as anyone the profound connection between our individual attitudes and orientations toward life and the material conditions of life that help shape those attitudes and orientations. Marx is commonly considered a materialist, yet what this means is not well understood. Marx is often accused of denying any possibility of the existence of a spiritual realm, affirming instead that the earthly material realm is all that there is. But Marx's metaphysics is actually much more complicated than this. Specifically, he is a materialist in the sense of understanding that humans do not develop ideas out of thin air. Ideas, thoughts, and orientations toward life are indelibly linked to the social, political, and economic structures in which people live. People may make structures, but at the same time it is also true that structures make people. This point is ably demonstrated by the well-known literary theorist Terry Eagleton in his provocative defense of Marxism titled *Why Marx Was Right*.

Eagleton observes that over long periods of time, structural institutional changes in a society can have a profound effect on human attitudes. Almost every reform that history has achieved in the criminal justice system was bitterly resisted when it was first introduced, according to Eagleton. Yet today, we would be revolted by the kinds of penalties meted out to lawbreakers in the past. Today, we would not stand for seeing even our most abhorrent criminals subjected to public flogging and hanging, or being burned at the stake, preferring the more "humane" lethal injection as the preferred form of capital punishment. Eagleton writes, "What really alters our view of the world is not so much ideas, as ideas which are embedded in routine social practice. If we change that practice, which may be formidably difficult to do, we are likely in the end to alter our way of seeing."[11]

To clarify this important insight, Eagleton offers several more examples:

> Most of us do not have to be forcibly restrained from relieving ourselves on crowded streets. Because there is a law against it, and because it is socially frowned on, not to do so has become second nature to us. This is not to say that none of us ever do it, not least in city centres when the pubs have just closed. It is just that we are a lot less likely to do it than if it were considered the height of elegance. The British injunction to drive on the left does not have to struggle in the breasts of Britishers with a burning desire to drive on the right. Institutions shape our inner experience. They are instruments of reeducation. We shake hands on first meeting partly because it is the conventional thing to do, but also because, being the conventional thing to do, we feel an impulse to do it.[12]

These examples are instructive even if they seem a bit trivial. But more substantively, Eagleton points out that "in medieval and early-modern Europe, avarice was regarded as the foulest of vices. From that to the Wall Street slogan 'greed is good!' involved an intensive process of reeducation."[13]

Returning now to our discussion of the islamization process, the political thrust often associated with Islam should not be understood as an attempt to spread the religion of Islam by state-sponsored coercion, but rather as a recognition that living a life of submission is very hard, and it can only be done effectively where the institutional structures of life are set up to reinforce this submission so that it becomes second nature—like handshaking, or not relieving yourself on the sidewalk! Trying to live a life of submission in the midst of institutional structures designed to promote greed, competition, and rampant materialism is well-nigh impossible. The structures have to be changed along with individual attitudes. This, I believe, is what the five pillars of Islam are designed to do.

11. Eagleton, *Why Marx Was Right*, 94.
12. Ibid.
13. Ibid., 96.

The five pillars are often thought to constitute the essence of Islam, the actions that define what it means to be a good pious Muslim. If you are not familiar with the five pillars, they are: confessing the Shahadah, praying five times a day, paying *zakat* (traditionally rendered as "almsgiving") to help the poor, fasting during Ramadan, and participating in the hajj, the pilgrimage to Mecca. All of the introductory textbooks on Islam will go into great detail describing how each of these pillars works. But few will have anything to say about the larger meaning behind these actions almost universally mischaracterized as "religious rituals." They are not religious rituals but rather the structural transformations required to institutionalize the idea of living in submission to God.

Take prayer, for example. Muslims engage in ritualized prayer at five prescribed times during the day. But why? Why not just pray whenever you want, whenever the inspiration comes over you? Why ritualize prayer, normally understood as a dynamic interaction with the divine? In an ideal Islamic (or better, *islamic*) society, mosques would be located such that everyone would be within earshot of one. At each of the five prescribed prayer times, a call to prayer emanates from the mosque, calling the faithful to prayer. The first line of the call is the familiar *allahu akbar*, "God is most great." In response to this call to prayer, Muslims everywhere would uniformly stop what they are doing and engage in a short ritualized prayer that physically enacts the idea of submission to God through prostration. Five times during the day, the routine affairs of life are "interrupted" by the reminder that God is most great, that God is more important than whatever else you might have been doing when the call to prayer was issued. If you are at work, God is greater; if you are at school, God is greater; if you are engaged in a sporting event, God is greater. Muslim prayer provides an institutionalized framework for changing individual attitudes. Seriously engaging in this act of submission five times a day, seven days a week, 365 days a year in community with other people would clearly have a profound influence on inner attitudes and orientations. How could it not?!

To see this, consider the reflections of Daliah Merzaban, a busy news wire journalist who was having trouble fitting the five prayers into her hectic schedule. The idea of praying five prescribed prayers every day seemed utterly impractical and impossible to her. But then she decided to try fitting her life around the prayers rather than the prayers around her life and found that this "instantly removed a great deal of clutter from my daily routine. Since regular prayer promotes emotional consistency and tranquility, I began to eliminate excess negativity and cut down on unnecessary chitchat, helping me be more focused, productive and patient."[14] She realizes that to an outsider the Muslim prayers can seem a bit obsessive. Yet in her experience, "the more time I devote to God, the greater the peace of mind I find filling my life and the more focused I become on what is important—such as treating my family and friends honorably, working hard on my job, giving charity with compassion and generosity, and maintaining integrity."[15]

As I noted earlier, Muslim response to my earlier book *Was Jesus a Muslim?* has provided me with the opportunity to speak in a number of mosques scattered across the country. While America is far from an ideal Islamic (or even *islamic*) society, I am constantly impressed with how seriously the pillar of prayer is taken in the American Muslim community. On many occasions, my speaking engagements have been "interrupted" by the prescribed sundown prayer. When this happens, little thought is given to first finishing the program and then praying afterward. Prayer, which is really the enactment of submission, takes priority over all else. When the time for prayer arrives, we briefly suspend the program and then resume it afterwards. Acknowledging God is clearly more important than listening to anything I have to say! I must say I have come to enjoy these "interruptions." They serve as a reminder of the larger context to what I am doing, which is obviously the point.

The third pillar, giving *zakat* to help the poor, is also an important way to institutionalize submission, but I will hold off the discussion until considering Islamic economics below. First, a word about the fifth pillar, the hajj. Every year, millions of Muslims from all over the world descend on the city of Mecca in Saudi Arabia. Here, this diverse array of Muslims engages in a number of interesting rituals, the details of which are beyond our scope here. The larger significance of the hajj is that it materially enacts the idea of the worldwide Muslim community living in unity in submission to the one God. National, ethnic, racial, and linguistic identities are subordinated to the idea that a Muslim's true identity consists of his or her common orientation to life—submission. The hajj is a truly powerful experience for Muslims. I was recently in the company of a young man who had returned from his first hajj. The impact on him was palpable. He was having a hard time reorienting himself to the mundane affairs of life, like his job. The hajj had lifted him up to engage the vertical dimension of life

14. Merzaban, "How to Pray."
15. Ibid.

in such a profound way that he was struggling to settle back into horizontal chronological time. In line with Terry Eagleton's Marxist insight, participation in this institutionalized process had fundamentally altered his inner attitudes and orientations.

Many of my mosque visits have been sponsored by the Islamic Organization of North America (IONA). IONA is a movement headquartered in suburban Detroit dedicated to the islamization of society in order to promote justice in the human community through living a life of submission. The organization's emir, Mustafa Elturk, and I make joint presentations on many of these mosque visits. In one instance, when we were visiting the very large Muslim Community Association of South Bay (in the Silicon Valley area of California), Emir Mustafa was invited to present the *khutbah* (sermon) during Friday prayers at the mosque. I had the privilege of listening to his remarks along with as many as six hundred other mosque attendees. Emir Mustafa challenged his listeners to consider why the five pillars of Islam are called pillars. What exactly are pillars for? Pillars, he declared, are only support structures. They are the foundation of a building, not the whole of the building. Likewise, Islam is not defined by the five pillars, as so many of the textbooks have it. The five pillars are merely the support structures on which the edifice of islam (submission) is erected. The pillars are the institutionalized structures that make living a life of submission possible.

Transformation of societal structures to support and reinforce the individual act of submission is, then, an inherent part of the islamization process. It is part of the genius of Islamic thought to recognize that human attitudes and fundamental orientations toward life cannot be changed via preaching and persuasion alone, as important as these are. Transformation of societal structures must be addressed at the same time. Few contemporary Muslim thinkers have made this point better than Sayyid Qutb, one of the foremost Islamic revivalist thinkers of the twentieth century. I realize that taking a positive view of Qutb is controversial in the West. As the primary intellectual engine of the Muslim Brotherhood movement in Egypt until his execution by the Egyptian government in 1966, Qutb is frequently viewed in the West as an Islamic fundamentalist whose writings have helped inspire Islamic terrorism, not least the actions of al-Qaeda. This characterization is probably unfair, but arguing against it is not my purpose here. I am interested in the way Qutb understands the well-known and fear-inspiring Arabic word *jihad*.

While being tortured in an Egyptian prison cell in the 1960s on what were likely trumped-up charges that he was trying to assassinate the Egyptian leader Gamal Abdel-Nasser, Qutb managed to pen a short book titled *Milestones*, which stands as his clarion call for the development of an Islamic revivalist movement. It was the revolutionary nature of this book that led directly to Qutb's execution. But in this fascinating little book, Qutb provides a unique approach to the concept of *jihad*. First let me clear up the common misunderstanding that *jihad* means Holy War; it does not. *Jihad* is, however, a very important idea within Islam. The word literally means "struggle" and is interpreted to refer specifically to all the ways in which Muslims struggle to bring into existence a world living in submission to God. *Jihad* can refer to the internal struggle of individual Muslims as they try to change their own attitudes and embrace a life of submission. But *jihad* also refers to the struggle to transform societal structures that interfere with people's ability to live in submission.

Qutb's contribution in *Milestones* is to recognize that the political, economic, and social structures of the present secular system—structures diametrically opposed to the idea of submission to God—are so firmly entrenched and reinforced by the use of power that transforming them can only be done through the use of power. Qutb thus developed a proactive and rather muscular interpretation of *jihad* to justify the use of power to challenge and transform the societal structures of the secular world that stand in opposition to submission. This is not a call to use force to convert people to the religion of Islam, for Qutb is adamant that people's attitudes cannot be changed by coercion. Rather:

> Preaching confronts beliefs and ideas while the "movement" tackles material obstacles. Foremost among these is political power resting on a complex of interrelated ideological, racial, class, social, and economic structures. These two approaches—preaching and the movement—in unison confront "the human situation" with all the necessary means to achieve their common goal. For the achievement of the freedom of man on earth—of all mankind throughout the earth—it is necessary that these two methods be employed simultaneously. This is a very important point and cannot be over-emphasized.[16]

What is often portrayed as the "politicization" of the religion of Islam—that is, Muslims' penchant for not being satisfied with simply preaching the

---

16. Qutb, *Milestones*, 48.

Islamic message but trying to transform societal structures—is really nothing more than a recognition that the Islamic message of submission cannot be fully engaged or—more positively—embraced without the proper societal support structures.

Qutb's radical call for a revolutionary Islamic movement is threatening to many, and he may leave himself open to the interpretation that he condoned violence (hence the link to terrorism) even though he never actually uses the word. But his insight that the structures of the secular world are themselves protected by force is unassailable. Qutb's own experience told him this—he was unjustly imprisoned and tortured when he criticized too many of Nasser's policies. But Qutb's is not the only word on *jihad*. A contemporary scholar and member of IONA, Ahmed Afzaal, has written an important little booklet that richly deserves a wide readership, *Jihad without Violence*.

Afzaal agrees with Qutb on the centrality of *jihad* in the Islamic tradition. Living a life of submission is difficult in a worldly system set up in opposition to such submission, and therefore, "Effort is required to resist and overcome the forces that pull us away from God, that lead us further from the path of God, be these forces within a person's soul or out there in society."[17] As a result, *jihad* should not be understood as just one out of a number of obligations that humans owe God—like one of the five pillars. Rather, "jihad is the ever-present struggle that underlies—and allows—the realization of any and all such obligations."[18] Where Afzaal parts company with Qutb and others is in strenuously arguing for *jihad* as a strictly nonviolent form of struggle to transform societal structures. In the contemporary world, where the legitimacy of most governments is tied to the consent of the governed, nonviolent forms of civil disobedience can prove to be very powerful means by which to bring about the kind of changes to societal structures that would render them more consistent with a life of submission. Because Afzaal understands Islam as denoting a particular attitude or orientation to life and not a specific religious identity, he recognizes, like Qutb, how essential the transformation of societal structures is to being able to fully inculcate those attitudes and orientations in one's life. You can claim a superficial religious identity in any type of society, but it is much harder to fully adopt a deep orientation to life in a social environment

17. Afzaal, *Jihad without Violence*, 3.
18. Ibid.

diametrically opposed to it—thus the importance of *jihad* for Muslims (or muslims).

Another contemporary Muslim scholar who gets this is Farid Esack. Though he does not speak directly to the issue of *jihad*, Esack does recognize the problem with trying to construct Islam as a confessional religious identity. Esack lived in South Africa under the apartheid system, and he recalls how during the struggle for justice and equality, government officials would try to dissuade members of the Muslim community from engaging in anti-apartheid politics on the grounds that they were granted complete freedom of religion. They could pray freely, give the call to prayer, build mosques and religious schools, and try to convert others to Islam. What more could they want if they were being given complete freedom to practice their religion? Here, the construction of Islam as a religion was simply a governmental ploy to disempower Muslims and socialize them into acquiescence to an unjust and oppressive societal system, to which Esack responds, "If our worship is not linked to our lives and to people's suffering, then it becomes a safe part of religion, a part that all the decision makers in unjust socio-economic structures would want to encourage. The separation between this-worldly and other-worldly matters has never really struck a responsive chord in the world of Islam."[19]

Clearly, if Esack understood Islam to be a type of religious identity, he would have had little reason to argue so strenuously against the South African government's attempt to construct it as such. One could easily have practiced the religion of Islam while living under the oppressive apartheid system. But Islam is not a religious label for Esack; it is an orientation toward life that can only be fully engaged in a just and equitable societal structure. Thus, he underlines the "futility of personal piety in an exploitative society."[20] One cannot live in full submission to God when one is forced to live in submission to an oppressive and exploitative human power. Thus, being muslim requires one to engage in the struggle for social change. It is this recognition among Muslims—that people's attitudes are in part determined by the societal structures in which they live—that has led Muslim scholars to propose a specifically Islamic framework for economic life that they feel is unique and clearly distinct from capitalism and communism.

For example, the third of the five pillars of Islam is *zakat*, normally referred to as almsgiving or charity in most textbooks, though the textbooks

19. Esack, *On Being a Muslim*, 92.
20. Ibid., 94.

couldn't be any further from the truth. In Muslim understanding, *zakat* is not the action of giving charity to relieve the sufferings of the poor; it is a system of wealth redistribution designed to eliminate poverty and the very need for charity. More specifically, *zakat* is an annual tax of about 2.5 percent levied on accumulated wealth; the proceeds are to be distributed among the needy to ensure a minimum standard of living until they can become self-supporting and become *zakat* payers rather than recipients. Such a system would have the effect of regularly redistributing large concentrations of wealth in order to eliminate true poverty and ensure a life of integrity for all. As such, contemporary Muslim thinkers have developed what they view as a uniquely Islamic economic system with *zakat* as its foundation. This is not the place to go into a detailed discussion of Islamic economics. But it is important to note how Islamic economics functions as a mode of structural transformation designed to direct the attitudes and orientations of individuals away from an emphasis on the accumulation of material wealth as the primary purpose of life.

One Muslim scholar, Mustafa Mahmud, has made the striking statement, "Wealth is not sought for itself in Islam but is sought as a means to piety and a way to upright, merciful, and loving action."[21] Imagine standing up in an economics class at Harvard Business School and declaring that wealth is primarily a means to piety! You would be laughed right out the door and would probably flunk the class. We all know that wealth is not a means to something greater than itself—like piety. The profit motive is the engine of business and the accumulation of wealth the very point of capitalism. Wealth accumulation has, in America, become an end in itself. If wealth *does* in any way act as a means to something greater than itself, it acts as a means to power and prestige, but certainly not piety! But why do we think this way? Why does the mere suggestion that wealth may function as "a means to piety and a way to upright, merciful, and loving action" seem so absurd? It is because our attitudes toward money and wealth have been so thoroughly determined by the economic system in which we live, a system that enshrines competition for resources and the accumulation of wealth for its own sake as the fundamental economic values trumping all others.

But in an Islamic framework, where an attempt is made to live by an ethic of submission to a larger divine reality, it becomes critical that people be freed from the slavery of exploitative economic relationships so that

21. Mahmud, "Islam vs. Marxism," 130.

they can fully inculcate that ethic of submission in their lives. It is critical therefore to develop an economic system that will condition people's attitudes toward money and wealth in a way that leads to just and equitable economic relationships, not unjust, exploitative ones. This is exactly what Islamic economics seeks to do. According to the Muslim scholar M. Umar Chapra, since "social welfare has a place of absolute importance in Islam, individual freedom—though of considerable significance—does not enjoy a place independent of its social consequences."[22] Islamic economics is based on a fundamentally different value system than global capitalism.

When I teach about Islamic economics, my students' reactions are very predictable. They call Islamic economics impractical and strongly resist any suggestion that it could work in America. When I push them to be more specific about their assertions of impracticality, their reaction is again quite predictable. "It goes against human nature," they say. "We all know that humans are greedy by nature and would never stand for a *zakat* system that redistributed their wealth in such a big way." Come to think of it, Bill Gates might be required to pay an annual tax of a jaw-dropping $1.25 billion in a *zakat* system! And he might well resist (though Warren Buffett might not!). But what my students fail to consider is whether greed is truly an aspect of human nature or rather an attitude and orientation toward life that is conditioned by a societal system that requires greed for its operation. Could people's attitudes toward money and wealth be changed by living in a fundamentally different kind of economic system? Muslims definitely think so, my students' skepticism notwithstanding. This skepticism may simply be evidence of how thoroughly my students have been socialized by the prevailing capitalist system.

Where one has fully internalized an ethic of social rather than individual welfare, the paying of *zakat* might be done gladly. One's attachment to wealth as a means to power and prestige might well be transformed into an understanding of wealth as a means to piety and loving action in the world. People might actually be able to live according to the understanding that wealth is not owned, but merely represents a trust from God to be used for the welfare of all. But truly internalizing these values can probably only be done in the context of an economic and social system that reinforces them and makes them appear as "normal" as—to draw on Eagleton's example again—not relieving oneself on the sidewalk! Hence the importance of structural change in the islamization of society.

22. Chapra, "Islamic Welfare State," 246.

What, then, is the significance of this extended discussion of Islamic (or islamic) ideas for living a radically open life? How might living a life of submission to a larger power address the causes of anxiety and depression as Jung has laid them out? Though it may seem surprising, there is a very close connection between the two.

Islamic Thought and the Jungian Paradigm

As we learned in the previous chapter, Jung believed that anxiety stemmed from a view of life that had become too narrow and constricted. This constriction was caused, he believed, by living life entirely from the perspective of ego desire and forsaking any connection to the Self, what Jung envisioned as a mysterious constellation of energy arising from the depths of our psyches that represents who we truly are apart from the provisional roles we play. Ego desires stem from our superficial provisional identities and are tied to the sense of self we develop from the parental and societal contexts in which we have been raised. Ego identity does not represent our true identity, so trying to live in accordance with it over the course of a lifetime will naturally lead to anxiety and depression as the Self demands expression but the ego resists. The solution, according to Jung, is to let go of our ego identity (which essentially means giving up control over our lives) and connect to the Self as fully as one can, following wherever it wants to lead. This opening up of our perspective, both on ourselves and on life in general, allows us to grasp once again the reins of an authentic life, and anxiety and depression dissipate as a result. Recall how Jung said,

> I have frequently seen people become neurotic when they content themselves with inadequate or wrong answers to the questions of life. They seek position, marriage, reputation, outward success or money, and remain unhappy and neurotic even when they have attained what they are seeking. Such people are usually confined within too narrow a spiritual horizon. Their life has not sufficient content, sufficient meaning. If they are enabled to develop into more spacious personalities, the neurosis generally disappears.[23]

This all sounds wonderful in theory, but as I can attest, it is very difficult in practice. As a rule we do not give up our provisional ego identities easily. The Self represents mystery, a great unknown over which we have little

---

23. Jung, *Memories, Dreams, Reflections*, 140.

control, and most of us I suspect are afraid of our own inner depths. This is why we so much fear the silence of being alone and instead fill our lives with the noise, busyness, and superficial communication of television, computers, cell phones, and the like—anything to avoid being alone and in silence, where we might be forced to confront our own depths. It is much easier to try to remain secure in our superficial identities as long as we can, enduring the depression and boredom that result, so as not to face the tremendous anxiety associated with the loss of those provisional identities (though the anxiety epidemic in contemporary society shows that our coping mechanisms are not proving very effective!). Becoming radically open is hard work, and it is unfortunately made all the harder by the secular (and therefore religious) context in which we live, a context diametrically opposed to any notion of transcendence or spiritual depth.

In some parts of the world this process is made easier—though never easy—by a culture set up to encourage and support deep spiritual reflection and development. I repeat in a little more detail the example I touched on back in chapter 3: Malidoma Patrice Somé's autobiographical reflections described in *Of Water and Spirit: Ritual, Magic, and Initiation in the Life of an African Shaman*. Recall that Somé was born into an African indigenous tribal culture in Burkina Faso but as a child was kidnapped and moved to a Jesuit mission school where for fifteen years he was initiated into the culture of French Catholicism. Eventually, he escaped and found his way back to his tribal village; the elders would accept him back only if he underwent a series of elaborate initiation rituals that were dangerous and potentially life-threatening but that marked the passage from childhood to adulthood (though Somé was already in his late teens at the time and would normally have undergone this initiation at about the age of thirteen). Somé decides to submit to the rituals, and the rest of his book relates in detail his fascinating encounter with a spirit world where no meaningful distinction can be made between the natural and supernatural realms. Nature and supernature are for him one integrated reality.

In stark contrast to the cultural realm of indigenous Africa, modern Western society no longer engages in any kind of meaningful ritual of initiation into adulthood, leaving the superficial identities of childhood to linger long into one's adult years. Moreover, the development of secularism, as we have already seen, cuts us off from any engagement with higher time and locks us into a narrowly constricted chronological existence devoid of any connection to a larger spiritual realm. It is hard enough to connect to the Self when we believe that it exists. How much harder is it to connect to something that our secular worldview has banished from existence? So, not knowing where to turn, we take our anxiety and depression to the doctor's office. But instead of being told that we are on a spiritual journey to find our true identity, we are told that we have a physical illness caused by a chemical imbalance in the brain, and we are given medication. The support structures of modern Western society are completely inimical to any suggestion that there might be a larger realm beyond the material world to which we are connected through the deepest parts of our psyches. The mere suggestion is often ridiculed as childish or primitive.

Now, this rejection of spirituality is not necessarily a fully conscious or intentional act. Many people do feel the need for a spiritual orientation in the midst of a sea of secularism, so they go searching for it and eventually find the place where spirituality has been forcibly imprisoned by secularism: religion. Unfortunately, since religion itself is the creation of secularism and plays by its rules, it too loses a connection to spiritual depth and too often devolves into a series of superficial doctrines and empty rituals to which we cling for a sense of identity. Religion in the secular world comes to function as a Jungian provisional identity that serves only to reinforce a narrow and superficial view of life that enhances our anxiety and depression—and leads to a lot of societal discord and violence to boot. We can do better if we can only find some guidance along the way. And this is exactly what I think the Islamic worldview can provide. This is not to say that all Muslims are muslims, not by any stretch of the imagination. But I do think islam (though not necessarily Islam) can help point the way.

If the Jungian diagnosis is that we live with a narrow and constricted view of life fostered by our attachment to the secular desires of the ego—desires of fortune and fame—then living life from an orientation of submission to an overarching divine entity—Allah—and embodying that submission through rituals of physical prostration would seem to be a good way of suppressing such ego desires. As one Muslim woman put it to me, "You can't have your nose up in the air when five times a day it is pressed on the floor!" The whole islamic system embodied by the five pillars seems designed to create the kinds of societal rituals and support systems necessary to bring about an orientation to life that revolves around submission to a higher power and a larger context—an attitude and orientation the complete opposite of the secular attitude of ego fulfillment and material human flourishing. From an islamic perspective, our lives are not entirely our own. We live at the pleasure of an overarching power to which we owe our submission and which calls us to participation in a journey that is far bigger than what is circumscribed by our material earthly existence. We are called to live radically open lives in service to a larger story. Thus there is considerable resonance between a Jungian and islamic viewpoint. Not only was Jesus a Muslim, but Jung may have been one too! Now let me be absolutely clear here. I am not saying that Islam as a specific religious identity will save us. We don't all need to go out and join our local mosque (though you should not be afraid to introduce yourself if you are lucky enough to have a mosque in your community). Rather, it is islam as an attitude and orientation to life that just might bring us to a radically open life. In the next and final chapter, I will consider in detail what it might look like to live a life beyond the bounds of exclusive religious identity labels and radically open to transcendent power. What effect could such an orientation toward life have on each of us as individuals, and how could such a life positively transform an anxious, depressed, and unjust world?

five

Living a Radically Open Life

ONE OF THE MOST interesting aspects of the Qur'an is its penchant for making deep and profound observations about human nature that seem as relevant today as when the text came into existence fourteen hundred years ago. One such place is Surah 2:212:

> Enamored are the unbelievers with the life of this world, and they scoff at those who believe.[1]

If I didn't know any better I might think the Qur'an is addressing contemporary American society. Socialization into the philosophy of secular materialism has rendered the mere suggestion of the existence of a transcendent reality ridiculous to many people. We are so completely enamored with the life of this world that even God has been trivialized and reduced to nothing more than a guarantor of our material human flourishing: "Praise God and he will make you rich, or maybe even help you win the Super Bowl!" Of course, one reason we become so enamored with our material existence is because the secular drive to master the world, subdue its dangerous forces, and accumulate its many riches feeds right into the triumphant nature of our superficial ego identities, which in turn is driven by the deep psychological need to avoid giving up control to forces we do not understand and over which we can exercise no real power. Why live in submission to transcendent reality when we can simply ignore that reality and take perfectly good care of ourselves, thank you?!

Deep down, I believe we know we cannot really ignore the power of transcendent reality, and I think we really do desperately want to believe in

1. English interpretation from Ali, *The Holy Qur'an.*

its existence. We want to break out of the numbing effect of living entirely within the horizontal frame of chronological time. We want to connect to something bigger. We want to experience that place where life is, in Charles Taylor's words, "fuller, richer, deeper, more worth-while, more admirable, more what it should be."[2] So, to fill the void we *do* acknowledge God— by praying, worshipping, joining a religious community, and declaring ourselves to be Christian or Muslim or Hindu or Buddhist. In short, we become religious. And Americans become religious at a rate unparalleled in the West. But the more religious we become, the more anxious we get. Fortunately, we have now solved the mystery of this apparent paradox. The allegiance we pledge to exclusive religious communities that claim to possess unassailable answers to life's big questions in the form of enforceable doctrines and teachings are themselves the product of the secular frame from which we want so desperately to escape. Religion is a secular concept, so if life in the secular world is anxiety-producing, what chance will religion have to allay this anxiety?

We may have solved the apparent paradox that stands at the center of this book, but what do we do with this newfound knowledge? How can understanding the paradoxical relationship between religious identity and mental health help us live a more authentic—and less anxious and depressed—life? How do we live a life that is radically open? Unfortunately, answering this question will prove more difficult than accounting for the paradoxical relationship between religious identity and anxiety. The obstacles to living a radically open life—obstacles in the form of a dogged determination to hold onto our provisional identities, including religious identities, and the necessity of living within a societal frame positively allergic to any notion of spiritual depth or transcendent reality—are considerable and not easily overcome. In making the transformation to a radically open life, we are mostly on our own. In the words of James Hollis:

> Underlying the symptoms that typify the Middle Passage is the assumption that we shall be saved by finding and connecting with someone or something new in the outer world. Alas, for the drowning midlife sailor there are no such life preservers. We are in the sea-surge of the soul, along with many others to be sure, but needing to swim under our own power.[3]

2. Taylor, *Secular Age*, 5.
3. Hollis, *Middle Passage*, 95.

But going it alone does not have to mean giving up. We *can* buck the societal trend, if we really want to, if we can come to see how detrimental a secular materialist framework is not only in terms of our own emotional health but also in terms of its larger social effects. In what follows I will consider some of the resources that might be of help in overcoming obstacles to living a radically open life by transcending the religious identity labels to which we cling so dearly. Specifically, we must be able to overcome a fully materialist worldview, and we must develop a personal identity that transcends the restrictive boundaries of our provisional identities. Neither is easy to do, but neither is impossible.

Overcoming Materialism

The Jungian paradigm for human psychological development is based on the fundamental premise that there really exists a transcendent reality to which our psyches are connected at their deepest levels. But very few people take Jung seriously anymore. I'm sure this book will generate its share of ridicule (as the Qur'an predicts) for suggesting that Jung may have it right. After all, Jungian theory has largely been drummed out of the psychological establishment as human psychology becomes increasingly transformed into a scientific discipline centered on the workings of the material brain. Various psychological and emotional states are now considered to result from certain patterns of neural activity, and considerable resources are being poured into research to map the brain and learn how the brain generates our feelings and behaviors. How should we respond to this seemingly irresistible secularizing current that promises to reduce all of life to the random interaction of atoms, molecules, and energy? Is there really nothing more to the universe than stuff? Are those who believe in spiritual reality just the naive victims of what Richard Dawkins calls *The God Delusion*?

First, let's be clear. Secular materialism is a philosophical premise; it is not a scientific conclusion. No one, so far as I know, has devised a scientific experiment by which to prove empirically the assertion that the universe is an entirely material entity. Of course, while secular materialism cannot be proven scientifically, neither can the existence of spiritual reality. So adjudicating this question will require moving beyond a reliance on scientific investigation, though, ironically, science itself may assist in demonstrating its own limitations, as we will soon learn. Moving beyond science is a problem, however, in a secular society in which science holds the status of being the only gateway to truth. We have equated scientific truth with absolute truth, the implication being that whatever cannot be empirically verified cannot be considered real. I have no interest here in casting aspersions on the fruits of science and the scientific method. Science is a powerful tool for investigating the material aspects of the universe, and I find scientific theories fascinating for what they reveal about the nature of the material realm. The problem is not science so much as scientism, the philosophical premise that science is the only way to truth—a premise itself beyond scientific proof. Perhaps the first step toward becoming radically open is resisting this scientistic tendency.

But this is not easy. I know from experience just how difficult it can be. Before my bout with anxiety and depression, I never would have argued this way. I would not have boldly affirmed a belief in the existence of spiritual reality. I was thoroughly enmeshed in the secular framework and had real doubts about the existence of anything I could not see, hear, touch, taste, or observe with fancy scientific instruments. I was thoroughly secular in my outlook, and I too would have scoffed at the Jungian notion of the Self. But please don't miss the irony here. I wasn't anywhere close to being a professed atheist. I have been actively involved in church my entire life, and I even earned a Master of Divinity degree from an accredited seminary. I was religious and secular at the same time, and this is not an oxymoron. It is because I was secular that I was religious! I claimed a strong religious identity as a Christian, began to prepare for a career in the ministry, and even preached in churches on occasion, yet I was actually rather embarrassed to openly profess an authentic belief in God outside the walls of the church. The secular world scoffs at spiritual belief just as the Qur'an predicts. I was very much a functional atheist, outwardly professing belief in God (at least within the safe confines of the church) while unconsciously living according to the dictates of an atheistic materialist worldview.

Perhaps some of this goes back to my formative experience. My mother was a very pious churchgoer and made sure that my sister and I were raised in the church and attended Sunday school. Yet I distinctly recall how at home we talked little of God and rarely, if ever, prayed as a family, and Bibles were hidden away in drawers as if they were pornographic magazines! I learned early that it was expected, but also embarrassing, to be religious. I doubt my experience is unique. How many people who profess an outward religious identity harbor strong internal doubts about the existence of anything beyond the material world? I suspect their numbers are legion. How could they not be? The secularizing demand that religious faith be kept private trivializes the spiritual to such an extent that it is a miracle anyone even tries to believe anymore. How can we accept the reality of God at the same time that we profess belief in a God who has no relevance for anything beyond our own private spiritual lives? What happened to the sovereignty of God? I suspect there are many more functional atheists around than actual professing atheists.

For me, coming to believe in the existence of a spiritual reality to which I am connected at the deepest levels of my psyche only occurred through the process of the breaking down of my provisional ego identity and the resultant identity crisis that ensued. Despite the unspeakable pain associated with major anxiety and depression, it is this pain that has the power to lead us to a deep connection to transcendence and return us to life. This is why medicating away anxiety and depression can be so harmful; removing painful symptoms cuts us off from the very resources that can authentically save us. Provisional ego identities prove to be recalcitrant, and they do not give up easily. Even James Hollis confesses:

> I was in my fourth year of analysis in Zurich, obviously committed to the process, before it really hit home to me that there was an active place of wisdom, deeper than my conscious knowing, that had been speaking to me all the while. What an obvious recognition, yet how recalcitrant my consciousness had been. The trek from head to heart took four years.[4]

Connecting to the Self is not an easy or short process; in fact, it is the process of a lifetime. But it cannot even commence when we are so blinded by secular materialism that we fail to even consider the possibility of transcendence. Fortunately, there are reasons to consider it.

Earlier we encountered the idea that the sacred/secular dichotomy is a common social construction of the modern West; it is not a description of the way the world really is. It is now time to tackle another common dualistic structure that is almost universally taken for granted, at least in the modern West—the natural/supernatural dichotomy. We normally talk about reality in such a way that God is relegated to a realm beyond nature, and the supernatural takes on a negative connotation such that belief in it is by definition *un*natural and tantamount to superstition. And who wants to be branded superstitious?! Superstition is what we call the religious

4. Hollis, *Finding Meaning*, 254.

beliefs of "primitive" peoples. One way to recover a sense of the reality of a spiritual realm is to transcend this dichotomy and recognize once again the *naturalness* of spiritual reality. This may seem like a bizarre request, but a little research suggests that there are very good reasons for attempting this recovery. The charge that "primitive" peoples are superstitious because they naively accept the existence of supernatural spirits may be dead wrong.

In this regard, ecological philosopher and writer David Abram tells a fascinating story about the time he spent many years ago among the indigenous people of the island of Bali, where he had gone to investigate the medical uses of magic. Abram, who had been a magician himself once, was living in a small one-room hut situated within a larger family compound. Each morning, a woman delivered a plate of fruit to his hut for breakfast, which he ate while sitting outside watching "the sun slowly climb through the rustling palm leaves."[5] Curiously, every morning, he noticed that in addition to delivering his plate of fruit, the woman was also carrying several platters each holding a small pile of rice with which she daily disappeared behind the buildings of the compound. One day, Abram decided to ask the woman who the rice was for, to which she replied that it was an offering made to the household spirits. Really curious now, Abram decided to follow her, observing that she set the small platters of rice on the ground at the back corner of each building in the compound.

One afternoon, he walked behind his hut to check on the rice platters, only to find them empty. The next morning, after the woman brought his breakfast, Abram waited for her to deliver the platters of rice to their appointed locations behind the huts, and then snuck around to observe them. They appeared to be simply platters of rice. But as Abram tells it, "Yet as I gazed at one of them I suddenly noticed, with a shudder, that one of the kernels of rice was moving. Only when I knelt down to look more closely did I see a tiny line of black ants winding through the dirt to the palm leaf."[6] Before long an entire column of ants arrived and devoured the rice. Abram walked back to his room, chuckling to himself at the naivety of the natives. They went to such great trouble to daily placate the household spirits, only to have the offering stolen by ants! But then another thought slowly dawned on him. "What if the ants themselves were the 'household spirits' to whom the offerings were being made?"[7]

5. Abram, "Ecology of Magic," 307.

6. Ibid., 308.

7. Ibid., 309.

As Abram pondered the matter, he began to understand what was going on. The family compound, like many built on tropical islands, was situated in the vicinity of several large ant colonies. Since a considerable amount of cooking took place in the compound, ant infestations were a constant threat. The daily gift of rice strategically located on the outside perimeter of the compound seemed to have the effect of keeping the ants from entering the center of the compound. This created a boundary between the ant world and the human world, and "by honoring this boundary with gifts, the humans apparently hoped to persuade the insects to respect the boundary and not enter the buildings."[8] Abram still remained puzzled at first as to why the woman referred to the ants as household *spirits*, but came to understand how his puzzlement only reinforced how bound up he was in a specifically Western understanding of what constitutes a spirit—a supernatural entity frequently taking human form. The "spirits" of indigenous cultures, according to Abram, "are primarily those modes of intelligence or awareness that do not possess human form."[9]

Abram argues convincingly that for indigenous cultures, the "sensuous world"—the world that we engage directly with our senses—is understood as the "dwelling place of the gods, the numinous powers that can either sustain or extinguish human life."[10] There is no need for indigenous cultures to conceptualize a separate supernatural realm since for them the natural world itself is spiritually animated. It is alive with sensitivity and sentience. Abram believes that the tendency within the West to restrict sensitivity and sentience to humans "originated in the loss of our ancestral reciprocity with the living landscape":

> When the animate presences with whom we have evolved over several million years are suddenly construed as having less significance than ourselves, when the generative earth that gave birth to us is defined as a soulless or determinate object devoid of sensitivity and sentience, then that wild otherness with which human life had always been entwined must migrate, either into supersensory heaven beyond the natural world, or else into the human skull itself—the only allowable refuge, in *this* world, for what is ineffable and unfathomable.[11]

8. Abram, "Ecology of Magic," 309.
9. Ibid.
10. Ibid., 306.
11. Ibid.

The natural/supernatural dichotomy is merely a way of talking about the world; it does not describe how things really are. What is, is. If spiritual reality exists, it is just as natural as the world of atoms, molecules, and energy—the material and spiritual are integrated, not confined to separate realms. There is no need to artificially split off a supernatural realm from the natural world, and there is even evidence from science that doing so might put us at odds with the way things really are.

Secular materialists, as the name implies, view reality as an entirely material entity. All natural processes are, at their core, the effect of interactions between elementary particles, atoms, and molecules, nothing more. But what exactly is the nature of these particles, atoms, molecules, and the energy that flows among them? Are they really material entities? Many people undoubtedly visualize atoms, for example, as consisting of a small material nucleus made up of protons and neutrons with a cloud of very small electrons revolving around it—like a mini solar system. But modern physics tells a very different story.

Albert Einstein, best known for developing the theory of relativity, actually won the Nobel Prize in physics for a much less famous discovery— his work on what is known as the photoelectric effect. The photoelectric effect describes the well-documented phenomenon whereby a beam of light shining on some particular metal will generate a small electric current in the metal. Prior to Einstein's discovery, it was unknown how this occurred since light was understood to be a form of pure energy propagated by waves. Since electricity is nothing more than the flow of free electrons, scientists could not understand how waves of light washing over a material could dislodge electrons from their respective atoms and cause them to flow freely, leading to the observed electric current. Einstein solved this riddle by theorizing that light, rather than being a continuous beam of wavelike energy, might actually consist of a stream of discrete particles, or photons, possessing a specific quantity of energy. When a light beam was focused on a piece of metal, the photons bombarded the atoms in the metal with just the right amount of energy needed to dislodge the electrons and generate the observed electric current. So light actually consists of particles of matter. But not so fast; in other kinds of experiments, light consistently behaves in a way best explained by the theory that light is pure, wavelike energy.

What Einstein and others have accomplished is to render any clear distinction between matter and energy, particles and waves, problematic.

Out of this discovery was born the branch of physics known as quantum theory, which has fundamentally transformed how physicists and philosophers view the very nature of reality. A full discussion of the metaphysical implications of quantum physics is beyond our scope here, but a brief summary of what some have dubbed "quantum weirdness" is in order.

Numerous experiments following on Einstein's work on the photoelectric effect confirmed that it is impossible to make any clear or meaningful distinction between matter and energy. Whether we are dealing with light or electrons, both behave sometimes like waves of continuous energy and other times like discrete particles of matter. At the quantum level, nothing is one or the other; everything is both/and. This wave/particle duality appears to be a fundamental feature of reality. The material world in which we live—the chair you are sitting on, the book you are reading, even your own physical body—dissolves into a haze of quantum ambiguity at its most foundational level. The universe is not just a container of space filled with minute solid particles of matter. The universe is rather a seething cauldron of quantum ambiguity (the more technical term is *quantum indeterminacy*) that resists all human attempts to precisely describe it or visualize it. The macro-reality of our daily experience is built upon a micro-reality we cannot fully comprehend. Moreover, it seems we are not just passive observers of this strange quantum world.

The physicist Werner Heisenberg, who developed the famous Heisenberg uncertainty principle, demonstrated the idea of quantum indeterminacy by showing that it was impossible to simultaneously measure with precision both the position and momentum of an elementary particle. The more precisely you measure the position of an electron, the less precise will be your knowledge of its momentum (a measure of where it is going). So if you can determine where a particle is, you cannot really tell where it is going. And if you can tell where it is going, you really don't know with precision where it is! Hence, you cannot make accurate predictions of the future state of any quantum system. Stranger still, it is the very act of measuring a particle's position that changes its momentum and the very act of measuring its momentum that alters its position. We do not merely observe a quantum system; we help determine the future state of that system through our observation. We are active participants in the making of the universe!

From the perspective of quantum theory, the world of our everyday experience—the trees, flowers, and birds—are something of an illusion. How we experience the world is not consistent with the way the world really is in its fundamental nature. This may be a new insight in the West, but it is far from new to humanity. Ever since the time of the Buddha, Buddhist thinkers have been convinced that the world of our everyday experience constitutes an illusion that must be dispelled by engaging in the process of enlightenment. Buddhists are convinced that the true nature of reality is fundamentally different from what we experience in our everyday lives. The world is not made up of a series of discrete structures with their own unique essences. Rather the universe is an interconnected web of relationships in which everything derives its essence by virtue of its interrelatedness to all other things. According to the fourteenth-century Zen Master Dogen, "Delusion is seeing all things from the perspective of the self. Enlightenment is seeing the self from the perspective of the myriad things of the universe." These age-old Buddhist teachings are striking in their similarity to the insights gained from modern physics. Is secular materialism founded on an illusionary (or even delusionary) foundation?

Contemporary Buddhist scholars have also turned their attention to the problem of human consciousness. Secular materialism tries to explain the subjective experience of consciousness as essentially a side effect of neural activity in a material brain, as we observed in chapter 3. This is why medication is considered the best way to treat emotional disorders. But the material nature of human consciousness cannot be established scientifically, and serious researchers—Buddhist and non-Buddhist alike—are now positing a much more complex relationship between our minds and our brains than a reductionist approach allows. Buddhist thinker B. Alan Wallace puts it this way:

> For Buddhism the mind is all-embracing. It has no existence apart from appearances, and appearances have no existence apart from the mind. Even our concepts of space-time and mass-energy have no existence apart from the mind that conceives of them. Thus, there are no absolute objects or absolute subjects. Nor is there any conflict between mind and matter, nor does one hold a dominant position over the other. We may separate them at the conventional level for the sake of discussion, but no absolute dualism separates mind and matter. Like our face and its image in a mirror, they arise in mutual dependence.[12]

Jung concurred, writing, "Without consciousness there would, practically speaking, be no world, for the world exists as such only in so far as it is

---

12. Wallace and Hodel, *Embracing Mind*, 180.

consciously reflected and consciously expressed by a psyche. *Consciousness is a precondition of being.*[13] We must not forget that it is human minds that have created the science used to reduce the human mind to the level of brain biochemistry, so the view expressed by both Wallace and Jung of the all-embracing nature of mind in the universe has to be taken seriously, which Buddhists have been doing for millennia. Non-materiality may be the true nature of this vast universe we call home. The Jungian Self may be nothing more than a cosmic mind to which our individual minds connect at their deepest levels. For those who scoff at the reality of a spiritual realm, the joke might be on them!

Striking in this regard is the frank admission of David Barash, an influential evolutionary psychologist, on how difficult it is to empirically account for the existence of mind and consciousness. He brands the question of the origin of the mind the hardest problem in science. He writes, "But the hard problem of consciousness is so hard that I can't even imagine what kind of empirical findings would satisfactorily solve it. In fact, I don't even know what kind of discovery would get us to first base, not to mention a home run."[14] Barash's despair over solving the problem of mind and consciousness belies the fact that he seems to know the contours of a solution, for he describes himself as "an utter and absolute, dyed-in-the-wool, scientifically oriented, hard-headed, empirically insistent, atheistically committed materialist, altogether certain that matter and energy rule the world, not mystical abracadabra."[15] Yet despite this, he confesses, "I still can't get any purchase on this 'hard problem,' the very label being a notable understatement."[16] Perhaps the profound difficulty of accounting for the mind via the physical structures of the brain might lead to some epistemological humility, but Barash nonetheless concludes, "I am convinced that . . . mind arises from nothing more nor less than the actions of the brain."[17] So Barash is convinced of something he admittedly has no empirical evidence for—a brilliant example of philosophical scientism at work! Nothing will convince Barash that the mind might have an existence independent from the brain because his position is based on a philosophical bias, not on empirically verified science. Scientists rarely admit this so openly.

13. Jung, *Undiscovered Self*, 48; Jung's emphasis.
14. Barash, "Hardest Problem."
15. Ibid.
16. Ibid.
17. Ibid.

Now, all this talk of a non-material reality that appears to be consistent with the idea of quantum indeterminacy and supported by Buddhist metaphysics is admittedly abstract and raises the question concerning the status of the personal God of the Jewish and Christian (and to a lesser extent Islamic) traditions. Can we still believe in a God who addresses us on a personal basis? When asked about his view of God, Einstein gave the following interesting analogy:

> I'm not an atheist, and I don't think I can call myself a pantheist. We are in the position of a little child entering a huge library filled with books in many languages. The child knows someone must have written those books. It does not know how. It does not understand the languages in which they are written. The child dimly suspects a mysterious order in the arrangement of the books but doesn't know what it is. That, it seems to me, is the attitude of even the most intelligent human being toward God. We see the universe marvelously arranged and obeying certain laws. Our limited minds grasp the mysterious force that moves the constellations.[18]

Einstein rejected the idea of a personal God but employed the term "cosmic religious feeling" to describe the emotions he experienced when contemplating the mystery and grandeur of the universe. And for him this was not atheism.

Many Christians at least will find it difficult to relate to an abstract spiritual presence and will hold tenaciously to a personal, anthropomorphic God—the God of Abraham, Isaac, and Jacob, as the Bible puts it. Does becoming radically open require forsaking a personal God for an abstract spirit? I don't think so. What is important is not so much how we conceive of God but whether we recognize the level to which our conceptions are human creations that cannot exhaust the fullness of whatever spiritual force might be responsible for the universe and all that is in it. The biblical portrayal of an anthropomorphic God who talks to people, walks in the garden, gets angry, or feels compassion is human interpretation, not a picture of reality. If we remember this, I don't see any real problem with holding a conception of God as a personal being—as long as doing so does not blind us to the reality of a mysterious and ineffable spiritual power standing behind our conceptions. God will always be larger, deeper, and more mysterious than our limited minds can imagine. If it were otherwise, God would cease to be God. Humbling ourselves before the ineffable is key

---

18. Quoted in Jammer, *Einstein and Religion*, 48.

to becoming radically open. But how do we cultivate such humility when we are controlled by our stubborn, triumphant egos?

Transcending Provisional Identities

The second major obstacle to living a radically open life is the difficulty we have giving up the control over our lives that our nervous egos crave when faced with a secular materialist culture that celebrates human material flourishing as its highest value. Why would we want to cast off our provisional identities and open ourselves to our own psychic depths when we have no clue what the Jungian Self emerging from the shadows will demand of us? This is a real problem and explains why so many people in our superficial culture fail to embrace the spiritual development of the second half of life and end up battling anxiety and depression as a result. I have no magic formula for how to intentionally transcend provisional identities. We are not really in control of when the Jungian Self will decide to manifest itself in our lives. I can, however, offer some reflections to demonstrate why it makes sense to assent to the demands of the Self if and when it does appear.

As I observed earlier in this book, provisional ego identities function, at least in part, as anxiety-management systems. They provide for us a sense of identity (even if it is a dysfunctional identity!) that helps allay the anxiety of the identity crisis that would attend their loss. The ego tries to create the illusion that we are in control of our lives, that we are masters of our own ship. We determine what we will do and who we will become. And our collective ego works to create the illusion that we can domesticate and control the world of nature and bend it to our will. The problem is that none of this is true.

Humility demands that we confront the truth of our human predicament. We live at the mercy of powers quite beyond our control, powers that can decide to threaten our very existence at any time. The evidence is all around us, yet we so infrequently stop to contemplate its meaning. Tornados demolish entire towns in a matter of minutes. Earthquakes wreak unspeakable devastation in just a few seconds. Deadly viruses and bacteria roam the planet, continually mutating and thereby foiling the medications we devise to destroy them. The sun, which is the source of all life, will ironically also be the agent of earth's final destruction in a cosmic future of incomprehensible violence. The powers of nature, though magnificent to behold, are far from benign. We are not really in control of very much.

One need not accept the atheistic conclusions of Sigmund Freud to appreciate his depth of insight into human nature and the workings of the human psyche. Reflecting on the awesome power of nature, Freud writes, "With these forces nature rises up against us, majestic, cruel, and inexorable; she brings to our mind once more our weakness and helplessness, which we thought to escape through the work of civilization."[19] Part of the "work of civilization," as Freud describes it, is the development of religion, which Freud believed came about primarily to help humans cope with their powerlessness against the forces of nature. Freud offers three reasons people often give for why religious claims should be believed. First, our primal ancestors held religious beliefs. Second, we possess evidence for the religious beliefs handed down to us by our primal ancestors. And third, one must accept religious beliefs because it is forbidden to even raise questions about their authenticity (anyone who teaches the critical study of religion will know what Freud means here!). On this last point, Freud comments, "This third point is bound to rouse our strongest suspicions. After all, a prohibition like this can only be for one reason—that society is very well aware of the insecurity of the claim it makes on behalf of its religious doctrines."[20]

I think Freud has it absolutely right. The more firmly we hold to a particular set of religious teachings, forbidding all attempts to question them and denying that the teachings of other traditions have any value, the more we demonstrate just how insecure we are in the truth value of those teachings. There is a tremendous insecurity at the heart of fundamentalist religion, notwithstanding the claims of certainty espoused by many fundamentalist teachers and preachers. Who needs faith if one can have certainty? The problem is that certainty is unattainable. Ambiguity is fundamental to reality, as our previous discussion of quantum indeterminacy demonstrates. It takes tremendous courage to fully own up to this fact. Can we really break beyond the protective shell of our provisional religious identities? What value could there possibly be in doing so? If you can indulge me one more personal story, I recently had an experience that I think sheds light on this question.

While I was working on this book, my family and I went out one glorious, sunny, warm late June morning for a canoe trip on the Upper Iowa River near our home. This river is quite shallow and tame and not normally considered very dangerous. In fact, we had canoed it two years previously

19. Freud, "Future of an Illusion," 693.
20. Ibid., 701.

in August when the water level was so low that our canoe kept running aground. It seemed like we were out of the canoe dragging it over the rocks more than we were in it! So for this second canoe adventure, we decided to go in June when the water level was a little higher.

We were enjoying a wonderful day filled with wildlife sightings, the highlight being an active bald eagle nest. Shortly after a picnic lunch, we found ourselves approaching a place where many large trees had fallen into the river along the right-hand bank. Wanting to miss the trees, we maneuvered the canoe toward the center of the river, only to bump up against a small grassy island. The canoe began to rock, and the next thing we knew we were all in the water. While briefly submerged, I became aware that the water in this section of the river was fairly deep and I could not touch the bottom. My wife and I were not wearing flotation jackets, though thankfully our children were. As I struggled to get my head above water and look for my wife and children, I noticed the overturned canoe directly in front of me with my panicked daughter floating just to my right. I grabbed onto the canoe and instructed her to do the same as we rode the current directly to the downed trees along the bank. I was able to scramble up on a large horizontal tree trunk as the canoe became submerged beneath it. I then pulled my daughter up onto the tree trunk with me and let out a huge sigh of relief; I realized we would be able to climb the tree trunk up to the bank and get to safety.

As I collected myself and caught my breath, my daughter, still somewhat panicky, started yelling, "Where's Mommy?" As I turned to scan the river, my relief turned into sheer terror. My wife was nowhere to be found, and my son (just seven years old) was holding onto a vertical tree branch protruding from the water, only his head and shoulders visible. Seeing that the water was over my head and the current was strong, I knew if I jumped back into the river to rescue him I would be swept downstream away from him. I felt completely helpless and turned back to my daughter, uttering a totally obvious, "This is serious!" In an instant, a magnificent day transformed into a nightmare.

My son, who, surprisingly, was not panicking, assured me that he was unhurt and could hold on to the tree branch for awhile. His stoicism calmed me a little, yet I knew I needed to get help—and fast. Unfortunately, my cell phone was waterlogged and so nonfunctional, and I had also lost my glasses in the river and couldn't see very well. Still not knowing what had happened to my wife, my daughter (who was now barefoot) and I whacked our way through thick weeds trying to find a way out to a road or a house where we could find help, but all we found was a barbed-wire fence! Knowing I could not leave my son alone for long, we quickly returned to the riverbank, and I began planning my own rescue attempt, climbing out onto another downed tree that was a little closer to where my son was. As I was trying to develop a workable rescue plan, a man magically appeared out of the trees on the opposite bank. As I frantically called for help, he immediately responded that police and fire rescue were on the way and that my wife was well downstream but unhurt.

I later learned that when the canoe tipped over, my wife had grabbed onto a loose flotation jacket (that we were using as a seat cushion!) and our small cooler and used these as flotation devices. The current, rather than driving her to the tangle of trees with the rest of us, instead drove her downstream. She was eventually taken into a different tangle of trees from which she had to extricate herself, and then came to a shallower part of the river near an overpass where she was able to flag down assistance. Of course, just as we had no knowledge of her whereabouts or condition, she had no idea what had become of any of us. This experience was a truly terrifying one for all of us.

Eventually, the police and fire departments arrived, and my son was rescued by three firefighters tied together and anchored to the bank by ropes. Seeing this coordinated effort, I was greatly relieved that I did not need to attempt this rescue by myself. I might have gotten us both killed! After a brief stay in the emergency room, where my son was treated for mild hypothermia, we returned home unharmed and grateful for how lucky we had been. Only three days later we heard a news story about a young man in Waterloo, Iowa, who jumped into the Cedar River to help two struggling children, only to drown in the attempt (the children were rescued by someone else)! We understood just how dangerous even a shallow river can be and realized how many really bad things could have happened to us. We were truly fortunate.

Now, my purpose for relating this story is not to brag about our good fortune, as grateful as we are for it. I tell it first to emphasize how true it is that we all live at the mercy of forces over which we have little control—how helpless and powerless we truly are in the face of the powers of nature that surround us. Any one of us—or all four of us—could easily have drowned in the river that day or at least been seriously injured. Nature, while profoundly beautiful, is also profoundly dangerous. This would have been lesson enough, yet from this experience I gained another, more surprising insight.

In the midst of all the panic, terror, and helplessness I experienced at seeing my son in a potentially life-threatening situation from which I feared I could not save him, and at not knowing whether my wife was alive, dead, or seriously hurt, I felt strangely alive in a way that I rarely ever feel when I am safe, secure, and going about the daily affairs of my life. In the midst of what felt to me like a life-and-death struggle, I was lifted out of the framework of ordinary chronological time and into higher time. A vertical dimension opened up, and I experienced a magnificent surge of aliveness even in the midst of the terror. It may be that we become most alive when we find ourselves closest to our own vulnerabilities. In this situation, like it or not, we are forced to become radically open—to have all our provisional identities swept away and to see our lives in their organic totality. When we face the real and immediate prospect of our own annihilation, the superficial concerns of our provisional ego identities no longer carry much meaning. The powers of nature could care less what religion we practice. Perhaps this is why an identity crisis feels so much like death. We become most alive in the face of our own mortality because then, just to survive, we are forced to connect to an enlarged framework for our existence.

The irony here is that we possess, like all creatures, a biological drive to preserve our existence when it is threatened. But unlike other creatures who really can't control the powers that threaten them, we humans have the unique ability to arrange our surroundings to try to create at least the illusion of safety, security, and invulnerability. We build houses, cities, and all kinds of artificial environments to insulate us from the natural environments against whose powers we stand helpless. We develop medical science to fight back against the viruses and bacteria that would do us in and devise all kinds of technologies to keep ourselves alive as long as possible. Truth be told, we have been quite successful at this manipulation, but there is a real price to pay. By insulating ourselves from the powers that threaten us, we separate ourselves from the wellspring of authentic life, and boredom, depression, and anxiety are the unpleasant result. This double-edged sword of human culture is brilliantly outlined in Freud's *Civilization and Its Discontents*. I would venture to guess that anxiety and depression are not major problems in indigenous cultures where people live out the struggle for existence every day, intimately connected to the powerful forces of nature. Indigenous peoples live in constant connection to higher time.

No matter how hard it may be, rejecting secular materialism and transcending provisional identity are keys to alleviating the boredom, depression, and anxiety that plague our lives in the secular world. It is truly in our own best interest to develop radically open lives, but there may also be benefits that go beyond our individual emotional well-being. Living radically open lives—and, specifically, transcending religious identity—holds the promise of creating a more humane collective life as well.

The Struggle for Justice

Since religion and its correlate, religious identity, are the creations of the secular world, we should not be surprised to find that religions today exercise little influence over the collective affairs of life, especially the collective affairs that fundamentally determine the most important contours of life—political and economic affairs. The secular demand that our spiritual sensibilities, to the extent we still have them, be privatized, leaving behind a supposedly value-neutral secular public space, increasingly renders religion a trivial and banal concept. We may pray and worship on Sunday (or Friday or Saturday), but the important affairs of our collective lives must be conducted without any reference to a transcendent reality. We absurdly profess belief in an all-powerful God, only to turn around and severely limit which aspects of life this God is allowed to influence, thus making a mockery of the very idea of divine sovereignty and omnipotence. One cannot restrict the realm of God's influence without claiming sovereignty for oneself. If God is God, then it is not for us to decide what God can and cannot be in charge of.

As absurd as it is, this desire to restrict God's influence over the collective affairs of life has been enshrined in the outrageously banal doctrine of the separation of church and state. Resistance to the absurdity of this attempted separation is clearly evidenced by the movement so common today among evangelical Christians to usurp the political process in support of a narrow religious agenda. On the one hand, the attempt to bring God back into the political process *is* actually more intellectually coherent than the separationist position advocated by the alliance between moderate Christians and secular liberals. But please do not misunderstand me. I do not support this evangelical mission despite its greater intellectual coherence because evangelical Christianity has devolved to such a great extent into a provisional religious identity devoid of any real connection to a deep or mature spirituality that it is incapable of truly bridging the sacred/secular divide. Evangelicals would merely replace one human-created secular institution—the state—with another human-created secular institution—the church.

Perhaps more disturbing is the extent to which mainline Christian denominations support church-state separation as a way to maintain the purity of religion. These Christians advocate for separation because they don't want religion to be sullied by the corrupting influences of the secular state, but in the process, being religious becomes for them simply an end in itself. Few religious organizations are more directly involved in the struggle to maintain church-state separation than the Baptist Joint Committee for Religious Liberty (BJC). Headquartered in Washington, DC, and supported by a large coalition of Baptist groups, the BJC actively lobbies for the maintenance of the proverbial "wall of separation" between the church and the state. Several years ago, commenting on a *New York Times* op-ed column titled "Give Them Some of that Free-Market Religion" written by Eduardo Porter, the executive director of the BJC had this to say:

> Porter rightly concludes that this free-market model depends for its effectiveness on a full-bodied understanding of the separation of church and state. To the degree that government participates in the creation of a religious monopoly, the competitive forces that have caused religion to thrive are undercut.[21]

Religion, in this view, has devolved into nothing more than a commodity to be marketed, bought, and sold in a free market of religious ideas. Religion is just one more commodity whose proliferation is enhanced by the competitive forces of the free market, and this proliferation of religion is understood to be a good in and of itself. In this kind of environment, it is hardly a surprise that many people shop for a church the way they shop for a car, test driving a series of congregations until they find the one they like best. But to what end is this proliferation of religion harnessed? What makes flourishing religiosity such an obvious good? This question is never asked.

A similar point is made by the influential Baptist scholar of religion Randall Balmer:

> Religion always functions best from the margins of society and not in the councils of power. That is the great lesson of American

21. Walker, "Bad Things Happen."

history—and, arguably, of all church history. Once religion han-
kers after temporal influence, the faith loses its prophetic edge.
The proper place for all believers, Baptist or otherwise, is on the
margins, calling the powerful to account, all the while refusing the
seductions of power.[22]

Balmer may be absolutely correct that religion functions best from the
margins, but he fails to ask the more important question: What good is being religious in a secular society when doing so trivializes the very spiritual
reality we profess to believe in and cuts us off from spiritual depth, leading
to anxiety and depression? That the free market of religious ideas under-
written by the separation of church and state has led to a proliferation of
religiosity in America there can be no doubt. But the flourishing of overt
displays of religiosity, as we have seen, actually contributes to epidemic levels of anxiety and depression. Being religious simply for the sake of being
religious is no bargain.

But religion does not only spell trouble for us individually. Confining
religion to the margins of society, as Balmer advocates, leaves the secular
forces of the triumphant ego free to organize all the economic affairs of
life around the goal of maximizing material human flourishing (though
rarely does this material flourishing extend to everyone). Don't believe me?
Just think back to the financial crisis of 2008. The ego-induced drive to
maximize profits on Wall Street through exotic investments like securitized
mortgages and credit-default swaps plunged the financial system into a
near collapse, and Main Street has been paying the price ever since in the
form of a depressed housing market and high unemployment, even while
the Wall Street barons are once again reaping huge profits. People worry
about regulating Wall Street to prevent these excesses. But what we really
need is the kind of internal regulation that would result from the bank-
ers transcending their provisional ego identities to live lives of submission
to the reality of transcendent power. This is at least the solution provided
by Islamic economics, but don't hold your breath waiting for it to happen
anytime soon.

Separation of church and state has, unfortunately, been underwriting
the maintenance of unjust economic relationships for a long time; today's
situation is nothing new. Back in 1886, a group calling itself the Central
Committee for Protecting and Perpetuating the Separation of Church

---

22. Balmer, "In Search of Baptists."

and State published a tract containing the following almost unbelievable statement:

> The appropriate spheres of the State and Church have, perhaps, generally not been clearly apprehended. The duty of the State is to protect its Citizens, to preserve Order, and to *dispense Justice*. The duty of the Church is to teach Religion and to *dispense Charity*. Charity, divorced from religion, provided for by public taxation, and dispensed by the State, loses its essential quality. It then becomes a certain and secure provision which society makes for its unfortunate and pauper classes.[23]

According to this document, part of the reason for maintaining church-state separation is to make sure that the state does not transgress its bounds and think that it might actually bear responsibility for providing "certain and secure provision" for all its citizens. And we certainly would not want to deprive the church of the "essential quality" of Christian charity, now would we? Church-state expert Philip Hamburger maintains that the Central Committee for Protecting and Perpetuating the Separation of Church and State was supported by the late nineteenth-century capitalist magnates Astor, Rockefeller, and Vanderbilt. Church-state separation is a boon to the rich and powerful. It creates a value-free secular space where the ego is free to advance its interest in material human flourishing no matter what the cost to society as a whole. More and more, religion scholars are waking up to the role played by religion in the development of unjust economic relationships.

One such scholar is Timothy Fitzgerald. He claims that "the construction of 'religion' and 'religions' as global, crosscultural objects of study has been part of a wider historical process of western imperialism, colonialism, and neocolonialism."[24] Part of this process has been to establish what Fitzgerald calls an "ideologically loaded distinction between the realm of religion and the realm of non-religion or the secular."[25] What this does is to authorize the assigning of moral values to the realm called "religion," thereby leaving behind a secular realm of politics and economics that is now seen as value-free (since values have already been assigned to the other realm). Once moral values are confined to the religious realm, they become, in Fitzgerald's words, "objects of nostalgia." Values like truth, fairness, and

---

23. Quoted in Hamburger, *Separation of Church and State*, 307; emphasis in original.
24. Fitzgerald, *Ideology of Religious Studies*, 8.
25. Ibid.

justice indeed sound nice when encountered in church, but outside of the religious realm they are often treated as idealistic, as a utopian vision hopelessly out of touch with the vagaries of the "real" world. Justice sounds nice as a goal, but it is not very practical! In the real world of everyday life, economic and political systems are understood to operate according to a set of "value-free" scientific facts regarding the "natural world of autonomous individuals maximizing their rational self-interest in capitalist markets."[26]

But of course, as Fitzgerald recognizes, this supposedly value-free secular landscape is not really value-free at all. It too operates with a core set of moral principles, among them individualism, competition, and exploitation. In the secular world, the purpose of life revolves around competition for limited resources, accumulation of as much material wealth as possible, and exploitation of others when it is necessary to advance one's material interests. What the construction of religion does, however, is to obscure the moral nature of these secular values by treating them not as values but as scientific facts—as statements about the way the world really is. Since values are placed in the box called religion, the remaining secular space must be a realm of value-free facts. Value judgments can be challenged; facts cannot. What is, is. So if individualism, competition, and exploitation are simply descriptions of the way life is, then the economically exploitative society that results from these "facts" cannot be questioned or changed. The construction of a uniquely religious realm, then, helps maintain the unjust economic status quo. Or, in Fitzgerald's words, religion has functioned as part of a "complex process of establishing the naturalness and ideological transparency of capitalist and individualist values."[27]

In a fascinating little book called *Masking Hegemony: A Genealogy of Liberalism, Religion, and the Private Sphere,* Craig Martin shows how the rhetoric of church-state separation serves to leave value-laden discourses unchallenged, thereby leaving them in place where they can cause real harm to real people. When liberals cry out that evangelicals violate the doctrine of separation by basing public policy decisions on religious ideas, the liberals effectively tie their own hands because they cannot then challenge these religious ideas without themselves violating the separationist doctrine they hold to so dearly.[28] Forsaking the ability to challenge religious ideas that influence public policy then leaves these policies in place.

26. Ibid.
27. Ibid., 9.
28. Martin, *Masking Hegemony,* 157.

For example, during the struggle for civil rights in this country, Senator Robert Byrd of West Virginia contributed to a filibuster of the 1964 Civil Rights Act by reading the biblical text of Genesis 9:18–27 (the cursing of Ham) into the congressional record. Now, I am sure that secular liberals would argue that Senator Byrd had no right to base his public resistance to the Civil Rights Act on a religious text. This is a clear violation of separation of church and state. But by appealing to a separationist argument, the secular liberals gave up the right to challenge Senator Byrd's religious reasoning. What if Byrd's religious reasoning had, therefore, won the day and the Civil Rights Act had been defeated? Think of the implications for America! When public officials employ religious arguments in support of a policy position, what would be the harm of debating the merits of such religious reasoning in the political arena? Why not debate biblical interpretation on the floor of the U. S. Senate? This suggestion may come across as absurd, but that just reinforces how blinded we have been by the myth of church-state separation.

The doctrine of church-state separation is therefore an ideological construction that can be used to support the continuation of oppressive economic, political, or social systems that in the case of economics is rapidly reducing all of life to the dehumanizing level of material accumulation (at least for those in the position to do the accumulating!). We can all practice our religion just so long as we do not expect those "religious" values to influence the political or economic system. Church-state separation trivializes religion by forbidding its influence in the most important affairs of our collective life, the unfortunate result being that some of us end up materially poorer while all of us end up spiritually poorer. When we meekly acquiesce to this system by holding fast to our exclusive claims to religious identity, we participate in the rapid dehumanization of our society and, increasingly, the world. Religion is not only a problem for our individual mental health; it spells disaster also for our collective societal health. Becoming radically open by transcending religious identity may be the best thing we can do for the entire planet.

But this will require breaking free of our triumphant egos and availing ourselves of the luxury of connection to the mysteries lying deep within our magnificent psyches. The fascination today with the accumulation of wealth at all costs both by corporations and individuals stands as a monument to the triumph of the human ego. We are now in need of a collective Middle Passage—a breaking down of ego identity and connection to the

Jungian Self. It is there we will find the internal resources necessary to truly reclaim our humanity. It is there we will find the wisdom of the cosmos filling our ears with a message of enlargement. It is there we will connect to the larger cosmic story in which it is our privilege to participate. It is here, in this enlarged vision of the magnificence of our lives, that we will find the solution to our boredom, anxiety, and depression—it is here, in the mysterious depths of our own psyches, not in the superficial concerns of our provisional religious identities.

Embracing Mystery

The move to radically expand our perspective on life and connect to the larger story of the universe is well captured by the early twentieth-century Austrian poet Rainer Maria Rilke in this oft-repeated line:

> I live my life in ever-widening circles that stretch out across
> the things of the world.[29]

Like the expanding ripples of a stone thrown into a pond, our awareness of the largeness of life should keep expanding outward over the course of a lifetime. But in too many cases this fails to occur, and instead we become imprisoned in an artificially narrow and constricted worldview. For ecopsychologist Anita Barrows, this imprisonment results in part from late twentieth-century theories of psychological development having arisen primarily in urban contexts where the social interaction between humans is the only thing considered important. Barrows wants to expand the boundaries of this ever-widening circle beyond the social world of human relationships to the world of nature and our interrelatedness to the more-than-human world. Any theory of psychological development "must take into consideration that the infant is born into not only a social but an ecological context."[30] I thoroughly agree, but we cannot stop at the boundaries of our ecological contexts. The contours of our awareness must keep expanding until they become as large as the universe itself.

It is really quite astonishing how little time most people spend contemplating the unimaginable grandeur of the universe that forms the real context for the human adventure. How easily we ignore our participation in a fourteen-billion-year-old cosmic narrative whose story line we barely

29. My own translation from the German text cited in Hutchinson, *Book of Hours*, 2.

30. Barrows, "Ecopsychology of Child Development," 103.

know and can only sketch in its broadest outline. Do we really think that the vagaries of our mundane, routine lives fully circumscribe the boundaries of our existence? Sadly, many of us do. Yet the truth is entirely contrary. Many of us undoubtedly engage the largeness of the universe intellectually—we may look up at the night sky and recite the names of the various constellations, identifying the Big Dipper or Orion's belt. But do we open ourselves to the full emotional impact of the dizzying incomprehensibility of it all? Generally, we don't, and I suspect the reason is similar to our reticence to engage our own psychic depths—fear of mysterious powers we do not control.

A couple of years ago, I was trying to help my daughter understand the scale of the solar system she was learning about in school. I thought that perhaps we could build a scale model by shrinking the sun down to the size of a basketball. The futility of such an attempt soon became apparent when my back-of-the-envelope calculations revealed that our model earth would be represented by a pea placed nearly one hundred feet away, with the outer reaches of the solar system two-thirds of a mile down the road! Even with a sun the size of a basketball, the nearest star would be twenty-four million miles away! I gave up even trying to calculate the distance to the farthest galaxies or quasars. Our lives are embedded within a cosmic story of effectively infinite magnitude, one that we are privileged to participate in just by virtue of being born. The universe is not a mere static backdrop against which our more important human affairs play out; our human journey is intimately intertwined with a larger cosmic narrative of which we are not the author. As the late Carl Sagan so famously put it, "We are star stuff." Though we often treat Sagan's saying as a cliché, it is not. The very atoms that make up your body and mine were cooked up in the nucleus of a faraway star that no longer exists. We truly embody the very universe that created us.

We should remember that the narrative arc of scientific discovery has entailed a systematic decentering of the human ego and opening up of larger fields of vision. In the ancient world, the earth was at the center of a rather small universe, but Copernicus and Galileo expanded our view and moved the earth away from its privileged position. Later discoveries transformed our sun into just an ordinary star among billions of others in an ordinary galaxy, which itself is just one among billions of other galaxies. The framework of our awareness has never stopped expanding along with a universe that, ironically, itself is expanding. For a while we could maintain our belief in the human being as a unique creation of God, but then Darwin took even that away. Now that we know that the evolution of planetary systems around stars is a regular process of the universe, and given the vast size and scope of the universe, the odds are good that life exists elsewhere; it is not unique to earth. The scale of the true cosmic context of our lives is so much bigger than we normally acknowledge—if we can just radically open ourselves to it.

Contemplating the vastness and richness of the universe need not leave us feeling alienated or alone, for this larger cosmic process is truly our home. Brian Swimme and Mary Evelyn Tucker conclude their book *Journey of the Universe* with a triumphant note of hope:

> If the creative energies in the heart of the universe succeeded so brilliantly in the past, we have reason to hope that such creativity will inspire us and guide us into the future. In this way, our own generativity becomes woven into the vibrant communities that constitute the vast symphony of the universe.[31]

Ample evidence is mounting that the universe is not a sterile, impersonal morass of purposeless matter and energy. The universe rather demonstrates a penchant for ceaseless creativity, as Stuart A. Kauffman so fascinatingly demonstrates in *Reinventing the Sacred*. Some would even go so far as to see a cosmic mind at work. We may not understand it all, but we are nevertheless participants in this truly grand narrative, a privilege bestowed on every one of us without our even asking.

Connecting to this larger story will require a willingness to embrace mystery and abandon the fruitless search for certainty so characteristic of our age. The famous evangelist Billy Graham repeatedly asked the throngs of people who flocked to his crusades, "If you die tonight, are you certain that you will go to heaven?" Playing on people's doubt, Graham then invited the crowds to certainty through a public acceptance of Jesus Christ. But this type of certainty is an illusion. No one really knows what happens when we die. Recall that Jung referred to life as "a luminous pause standing between two mysteries which as yet are one."[32] Our births are enshrouded in mystery; not one of us had anything to do with our being here. We just arrive in this world helpless and completely ignorant of why we are here or what it all means. And death is the great existential mystery about which

---

31. Swimme and Tucker, *Journey of the Universe*, 118.

32. Jung, *Letters*, 483.

we know very little. But in between, we have the privilege of participating in the grand process of the universe. Note that Jung calls life a *luminous* pause. We are lights in the cosmic narrative.

Embracing mystery will entail resisting the temptation—all too human—to demystify God or the gods and to reconstruct God as an anthropomorphized superhuman being. All constructions of God are human creations and cannot be taken as absolute representations of who God really is or what God really wants from us. Likewise, strong atheistic affirmations of the nonexistence of God or the gods are just as much a human metaphysical construction that goes well beyond what any of us can claim to know. Perhaps the only intellectually honest position regarding the existence of God is agnosticism—the affirmation that we cannot know whether God exists or not. I realize agnosticism has a negative connotation in the contemporary world, but it need not be construed in such negative terms. Agnosticism is simply an honest act of epistemological humility, allowing us to stand in faith in the presence of a mystery we do not understand. False certainty is the true enemy of faith, but doubt is its prerequisite. There is no reason why someone cannot be a faithful agnostic in the best sense of the term.

I find it quite surprising how reticent we are to embrace mystery. After all, mystery is the prerequisite for excitement (this is why people love to read a good mystery). How boring life would be if we knew what it was all about, if there was nothing new to discover. Clearly our tendency to deceive ourselves into a false certainty has led to boredom, depression, and anxiety. I am reminded of the pessimism of physicist Steven Weinberg's well-known dictum, "The more we understand about the universe the more pointless it seems." Weinberg seems to lose sight of the fact that we really don't know very much. More importantly, we can't know how much we don't know, so some epistemological humility is certainly in order. We truly live in the presence of mystery, and this is a good thing because a world of mystery will constantly surprise us with the novel, the unexpected, rendering life an exciting adventure. Besides, it is hard to be depressed or anxious while simultaneously feeling excitement! The two don't go together. Embracing the mystery of the cosmic narrative that frames our lives will lead to a sense of reenchantment of the world and an enlargement of our perspective that will go a long way toward diminishing anxiety.

This call for spiritually reenchanting the world, I realize, is not without controversy. Some thinkers have begun advocating for what they call secular reenchantment, which entails accepting the secular premise of the materiality of all existence but finding enchantment in the magnificent processes of this material world. For example, George Levine's *Darwin Loves You: Natural Selection and the Re-enchantment of the World* argues that we can find the enchantment we so desperately seek within a completely Darwinian understanding of the story of life, without appeal to any transcendent or spiritual reality. Levine has also edited an anthology titled *The Joy of Secularism* that contains essays similarly advocating for a secular reenchantment. I must admit that I find the idea of secular reenchantment to be rather curious and something of an oxymoron.

Levine and his colleagues clearly understand the damage done by secular disenchantment, and they recognize the need to resist the movement toward disenchantment. But at least on the theory of secularism I have borrowed from Charles Taylor, secularism itself is characterized by an attempt to understand all processes from within the parameters of the material world, and this attempt leads to disenchantment as we are cut off from a connection with non-material forces of enchantment. Calling for a secular reenchantment, then, seems to miss the point that secularism, almost by definition, is a disenchanting process. I wonder why it is so difficult for Levine and his colleagues to engage the possibility of a spiritual animating force at work in the cosmic story, even if we can't fully understand what it is or how it works. Have we really been so cowed into submission by the scientistic forces demanding that we accept as real only what is empirically verifiable? After all, even Darwin did not think his theory of natural selection necessarily undermined a religious worldview; toward the end of *On the Origin of Species*, he comments, "I see no reason why the views given in this volume should shock the religious feelings of any one."

The real lesson here is one of humility—developing the humility necessary to accept our ignorance and to openly engage mystery as mystery rather than trying to demystify it. We must practice *islam*—that is, submission to what James Hollis calls "the greater wisdom of the process." Of course, our egos will rail against the very idea that we are limited creatures, but seeking to transcend limits may be the fastest way to a life of meaninglessness. Some years ago at a conference held at Middlebury College, Ismar Schorsch, then the chancellor of the Jewish Theological Seminary in New York, challenged his audience with the striking statement, "Meaning is found in limits." If we came to a place where we could have an unlimited supply of anything we wanted, says Schorsch, nothing would mean anything. To see how right he is, consider the human quest for immortality. Contemplate what it would mean if we successfully conquered death. Close your eyes and try to visualize your life streaming off into the future as an unending succession of days! The prospect is mind-numbing. Without an end, life would cease to take the shape of a story; it would lose its narrative arc and devolve into a state of numbing meaninglessness. It is only because we are finite, because we cannot have all that we desire, because our choices matter, that our lives gain meaning. We must submit to our limited nature and accede to the larger wisdom of the process in order to truly find life.

Our true identity as human beings will be found in our enlarged role as co-participants in the cosmic drama of the universe. It will not be found within the narrow limits of the provisional identities we cling to so tightly. Among these provisional identities stand our claims to religious identity. But if my argument is at all cogent, these religious identities prove to be superficial; they serve to cut us off from our psychic depths where we might find our connection to the larger cosmic story—and this leaves us vulnerable to anxiety and depression. We need to become radically open by transcending those religious identities to become truly alive and fully human.

Please don't misunderstand me. I am not suggesting that we abandon church, mosque, synagogue, or temple, but rather that we resist the temptation to cling to an exclusive adherence to a single tradition as defining who we really are. I remain today a member of a church whose services I attend regularly. I serve on this church's missions committee, teach an occasional Sunday school class, and even preach now and then when the minister is out of town. But I also attend and actively participate in a Friday prayer service started by Luther College's Muslim Student Association, and I remain very interested in aspects of Buddhist meditation. What is my religious identity? It doesn't matter. Religion is not an identity to me. I am a child of the universe, and the various religious traditions are important to me only insofar as they contain resources that might guide and direct me toward that larger understanding of my identity—and one finds that all of them do contain such resources, if only one allows them to speak. Back when I claimed a strong religious identity for myself, I was essentially a functional atheist. Now that I don't claim a particular religious identity, I have become a faithful agnostic. My sense of the existence of spiritual reality is much stronger now that I have transcended a provisional religious identity and radically opened myself to the greater mystery.

I recently saw the following bumper sticker:

Trust those who seek truth; doubt those who claim to have found it.

What profound wisdom! I think it sums up everything I have tried to say in this book. I am trying every day to live a radically open life in willing submission to a larger mystery that I neither understand nor control. Engaging with mystery is at times unsettling, but opening up to its creative possibilities is also exciting and can at times be downright exhilarating. And I find that I am a whole lot less anxious. Do I still miss my mother? Of course, and I suspect I always will. But this is offset by the recognition that I live now in service to a reality much larger than myself; all I can do is willingly surrender in faith and trust to this reality. This is what it means to live radically open, to be full participants in the cosmic journey of the universe.

Bibliography

Abram, David. "The Ecology of Magic." In *Ecopsychology: Restoring the Earth, Healing the Mind*, edited by Theodore Roszak et al., 301–15. San Francisco: Sierra Club, 1995.

Afzaal, Ahmed. *Jihad without Violence*. Warren, MI: Islamic Organization of North America, 2010.

Ali, Abdullah Yusuf. *The Holy Qur'an: Text, Translation, and Commentary*. Elmhurst, NY: Tahrike Tarsile Qur'an, 2001.

Asad, Muhammad. *The Message of the Qur'an*. Bristol, UK: Book Foundation, 2003.

Balmer, Randall. "In Search of Baptists." *Report from the Capital* 62 (August 2007).

Barash, David. "The Hardest Problem in Science?" *The Chronicle of Higher Education*, October 28, 2011. Online: http://chronicle.com/blogs/brainstorm/the-hardest-problem-in-science/40845.

Barrows, Anita. "The Ecopsychology of Child Development." In *Ecopsychology: Restoring the Earth, Healing the Mind*, edited by Theodore Roszak et al., 101–10. San Francisco: Sierra Club, 1995.

Brodeur, Patrice C. " Religion." In *The Encyclopedia of the Qur'an*, edited by Jane Damman McAuliffe, 4:395–98. Leiden: Brill, 2004.

Chapra, M. Umar. "The Islamic Welfare State." In *Islam in Transition: Muslim Perspectives*, edited by John J. Donahue and John L. Esposito, 242–48. 2nd ed. New York: Oxford University Press, 2007.

Chidester, David. *Savage Systems: Colonialism and Comparative Religion in Southern Africa*. Charlottesville: University Press of Virginia, 1996.

Donner, Fred M. *Muhammad and the Believers: At the Origins of Islam*. Cambridge: Belknap, 2010.

Durkheim, Emile. *The Elementary Forms of the Religious Life*. Translated by Joseph Ward Swain. New York: Free Press, 1965.

Eagleton, Terry. *Why Marx Was Right*. New Haven: Yale University Press, 2011.

Esack, Farid. *On Being a Muslim: Finding a Religious Path in the World Today*. Oxford: Oneworld, 1999.

Fitzgerald, Timothy. *The Ideology of Religious Studies*. New York: Oxford University Press, 2000.

Freud, Sigmund. "The Future of an Illusion." In *The Freud Reader*, edited by Peter Gay, 685–722. New York: Norton, 1989.

Greenberg, Gary. *Manufacturing Depression: The Secret History of a Modern Disease*. New York: Simon & Schuster, 2010.

Hamburger, Philip. *Separation of Church and State*. Cambridge: Harvard University Press, 2002.

Hollis, James. *Finding Meaning in the Second Half of Life: How to Finally Grow Up*. New York: Gotham, 2006.

———. *The Middle Passage: From Misery to Meaning in Midlife*. Toronto: Inner City, 1993.

The Holy Bible: New Revised Standard Version. Nashville: Thomas Nelson, 1989.

Hutchinson, Ben, editor. *Rainer Maria Rilke's The Book of Hours*. Translated by Susan Ranson. Rochester, NY: Camden House, 2008.

Jammer, Max. *Einstein and Religion*. Princeton: Princeton University Press, 1999.

Jung, C. G. *Letters*. Vol. 1, *1906–1950*. Translated by R. F. C. Hull. Princeton: Princeton University Press, 1973.

———. *Memories, Dreams, Reflections*. Translated by Richard and Clara Winston. New York: Vintage, 1965.

———. *The Undiscovered Self*. Translated by R. F. C. Hull. New York: Signet, 1957.

Kauffman, Stuart A. *Reinventing the Sacred: A New View of Science, Reason, and Religion*. New York: Basic Books, 2008.

Kiser, John W. *Commander of the Faithful: The Life and Times of Emir Abd el-Kader*. Rhinebeck, NY: Monkfish, 2008.

Levine, George. *Darwin Loves You: Natural Selection and the Re-enchantment of the World*. Princeton: Princeton University Press, 2006.

Levine, George, editor. *The Joy of Secularism: Eleven Essays for How We Live Now*. Princeton: Princeton University Press, 2011.

Mahmud, Mustafa. "Islam vs. Marxism." In *Islam in Transition: Muslim Perspectives*, edited by John J. Donahue and John L. Esposito, 128–32. 2nd ed. New York: Oxford University Press, 2007.

Martin, Craig. *Masking Hegemony: A Genealogy of Liberalism, Religion, and the Private Sphere*. London: Equinox, 2010.

Masuzawa, Tomoko. *The Invention of World Religions*. Chicago: University of Chicago Press, 2005.

Merzaban, Daliah. "How to Pray Five Times a Day with a Busy Work Schedule." *The Huffington Post*, November 28, 2011. Online: http://www.huffingtonpost.com/daliah-merzaban/how-to-pray-five-times-a-day_b_1103662.html.

Nelson, Portia. *There's a Hole in My Sidewalk*. New York: Popular Library, 1977.

Palmer, Parker. *Let Your Life Speak: Listening for the Voice of Vocation*. San Francisco: Jossey-Bass, 2000.

Qutb, Sayyid. *Milestones*. Translated by Ahmad Zaki Hammad. Indianapolis: American Trust Publications, 1990.

Sehat, David. *The Myth of American Religious Freedom*. New York: Oxford University Press, 2011.

Shedinger, Robert F. *Was Jesus a Muslim? Questioning Categories in the Study of Religion*. Minneapolis: Fortress, 2009.

Somé, Malidoma Patrice. *Of Water and Spirit: Ritual, Magic, and Initiation in the Life of an African Shaman*. New York: Arkana, 1994.

Sullivan, Winnifred Fallers. *The Impossibility of Religious Freedom*. Princeton: Princeton University Press, 2005.

Swimme, Brian Thomas, and Mary Evelyn Tucker. *Journey of the Universe*. New Haven: Yale University Press, 2011.

Taylor, Charles. *A Secular Age*. Cambridge: Harvard University Press, 2007.

Turner, Erick H., et al. "Selective Publication of Antidepressant Trials and Its Influence on Apparent Efficacy." *The New England Journal of Medicine* 358:3 (2008) 252–60.

Walker, J. Brent. "Bad Things Happen When Church and State Mix." *Report from the Capital* 59 (December 2004) 3.

Wallace, B. Alan, and Brian Hodel. *Embracing Mind: The Common Ground of Science and Spirituality.* Boston: Shambhala, 2008.

Whitaker, Robert. *Anatomy of an Epidemic: Magic Bullets, Psychiatric Drugs, and the Astonishing Rise of Mental Illness in America.* New York: Crown, 2010.

Made in the USA
Monee, IL
14 December 2019